Tuesday's Child

Kathy Evans

Gill & Macmillan

Published by Gill & Macmillan Ltd
Hume Avenue, Park West, Dublin 12, Ireland
with associated companies throughout the world
www.gillmacmillan.ie

© Kathy Evans 2009
978 07171 4622 2

Type design: Make Communication
Print origination by Carole Lynch
Printed and bound by ColourBooks Ltd, Dublin

This book is typeset in Linotype Minion and Neue Helvetica.

First published in Australia and New Zealand in 2007
by Bantam.

The paper used in this book comes from the wood pulp
of managed forests. For every tree felled, at least one tree
is planted, thereby renewing natural resources.

A CIP catalogue record for this book is available
from the British Library.

5 4 3 2 1

For Eleanor, Ceridwen and Caoimhe.
Because three is the magic number.

Contents

Acknowledgments

This book started within hours of Caoimhe's diagnosis, when, with mind reeling, I started pouring my thoughts, fears, feelings into my battered Filofax on my bedside cabinet, half-formed, random and crazed. I wrote them down because I didn't know what else to do; I was on a ward of mothers celebrating the ordinary miracle of birth, and my extraordinary experience was a jangling discord which rendered me silent.

Over the months, I kept writing and my first debt of gratitude is to Sally Robinson, former deputy editor (features), *Sunday Age*, who encouraged me to shape my ramblings into a series of features worth printing.

I was overwhelmed by the response from readers in different countries who had lived various versions of my own story; I found myself bonded to faceless strangers by a sharing of banned substances; namely, our deepest, darkest thoughts, and spurred into rummaging still further into the corners of my mind.

Over the months as I struggled to compress these thoughts into a book, I was particularly inspired by Helen Featherstone's *A Difference in the Family*, Rachel Cusk's *A Life's Work on Becoming a Mother*, and Michael Bérubé's *Life As We Know It*; three books which beautifully and painfully acknowledge the overwhelming task in raising a child, disabled or not.

I owe the UK Down's Syndrome Association a big thank you for their prompt responses to my frantic e-mails scrabbling for information. Also, Dr Ciara Stewart and her husband Dr John Bates for their professional help with the medical aspects of this work, and especially, Ciara, for the friendship and support you gave our family in those early months after Caoimhe's birth.

Likewise, thank you to Kate and David, Mary and James, our Australian 'family'; Alison for helping me make sense of it all; Lou for the birthing classes (I liked the bit where we got out the cake) and Annabel for being there on that magical night. You brought your love and a bottle of Rescue Remedy and you made Caoimhe's life precious, right from the start. I can't find the words to thank you, there's a lump in the way. Wild woman, you are painfully missed.

Caoimhe's life has two distinct parts; an Australian one and an Irish one. My thanks must also go to the Williams family for the love and support they have given us here in crazy, beautiful Northern Ireland. In particular Cindy, for her insightful comments on this manuscript, but more importantly for becoming Caoimhe's friend and ally.

I am grateful to my eldest daughters, Eleanor and Ceridwen, for their unwitting wisdom; their stories, their plays, their vibrant, secret worlds in which Caoimhe is always a welcome guest and an equal player. It beats any early intervention programme.

But mostly, I want to thank Conor, for his loyalty and un-shakeable belief in Caoimhe and in me as her mother. Writing is a lonely job, and without your endless cups of tea, your technical rescue service, your listening ear, astute editing skills and first class parenting, there would be no book. Caoimhe is lucky to have you. We all are.

But then you had a good role model, your own father and Caoimhe's papa, Brendan McCooey, to whose memory I also dedicate this book.

Chapter 1
Welcome to Holland

In everyone's life there is a defining moment, an event which gathers itself from the ether and delivers a short sharp punch to the unsuspecting passer-by; like being mugged at a bus stop. That was what Caoimhe's diagnosis was like. It wasn't so much finding out that she had Down syndrome, but the sheer unexpectedness of it. One minute I was in the dream-like state that is a rite of passage of every new mother and then, BAM! In a matter of seconds it was snatched from me and I was left stunned, and gasping for breath.

My partner, Conor, and I had thought long and hard about having a third child. We already had two delightful, headstrong daughters, who fizzed and crackled with life's static from dawn till dusk, and we wondered, somewhat apprehensively, what a third child would bring. Still, being a family of four didn't sit comfortably with me; I can't explain why, other than to offer the excuse that I see numbers in colours, and four is an unattractive shade of orange, like mushy baked beans. Five, by contrast, is a vibrant greeny-turquoise with a metallic sheen.

Anyway, the primal urge to reproduce, or whatever it was, eventually drowned out the small but insistent voice at the back of my mind, which banged on about lack of money and time, and on our first attempt, I conceived.

It's funny having sex to become pregnant; it's quite a different experience to the sex you have when you're trying not to get pregnant. There's a sort of grim seriousness to the whole business, a brisk roll-up-your-sleeves approach in which fun is frowned upon. It's as if the child is waiting out there in the hinterland and you have to do it politely and discreetly in case it sees. And then the act is done and the child has been teleported from the astral plane into the warmth of your womb. A new life started with a small, courteous bang.

But before we could even begin to marvel at our good luck and incredible fertility, things went awry.

For a start, one of those do-it-yourself pregnancy kits would only register uncertainty. There was a pink line, faint as a ghost, which appeared in the little plastic window but it could almost have been a trick of the light. I stared at it, willing it to get stronger, putting it down and returning to it with a vain hopefulness, because two days later it remained nothing more than a dilute watery stain. Then came a low nagging pain in the cradle of my pelvis, a jarring sensation as if it was being rocked too viciously in an attempt to spill the contents. A blood test by the family GP revealed the levels of hormone needed to sustain this exiguous life-form were rising at a snail's pace. My baby lay paused at the interface between life and death. An ultrasound at six weeks showed her, a tiny star in a vast black universe winking down at us from the monitor. Next to her, a puddle of grey spilled across the screen like the Milky Way. I was bleeding internally and a miscarriage looked imminent. A second scan a week later picked up the beat of Caoimhe's crude heart, scarcely bigger than a pinhead. It was barely more than half the rate it should have been. The ultrasound operator's face was solemn; this pregnancy was surely doomed.

Back at home Conor and I trawled the Internet, desperate for information that might prove this prognosis wrong. We were not reassured. One clinical study we found on embryonic heartbeats concluded the odds of survival were less than 5 per cent. We were devastated. Even at this early stage she was our baby. So I wrote her a letter and waited for the inevitable. I was scared because I'd never had a mis-carriage. I wondered how much I would bleed: would it dribble out like tears or gush scarlet as if I'd been uncorked? I imagined seeing Caoimhe, a velvety mollusc on a bed of loo paper, or worse, not seeing her at all; inadvertently flushing her away with the efflux. Anyway, it never happened. Instead, a vague sickness crept over me which grew stronger as the days passed. An eight-week scan showed a healthy embryo with a strong heartbeat and a 90-plus per cent chance of survival.

Statistics, they can bend your mind like Uri Geller's spoons. At eleven weeks we were offered the routine screen-ing tests for Down syndrome, including a blood test and an ultrasound scan to examine the baby's neck for excess fluid. After the tests, the odds would be calculated based on the results, combined with my age. If the risk was more than one in three hundred, we could go on to have amniocentesis, which involves a large and sinister-looking needle perforating the amniotic balloon and removing a sample of fluid for analysis. This procedure, we were told, carries a 1 per cent risk of miscarriage, and for me, a high degree of fear.

We said no. I am not a religious person but over the years I've developed some sort of godless spirituality, a belief in the human condition and all its frailties. Besides, we were still heady with the triumph of Caoimhe's survival. We talked proudly about our little fighter, our tough little babe. She could have had two heads and we wouldn't have cared. And, of course, we believed Down syndrome would never happen to us. For a start I was only 35, at the crest of fertility's slippery slope. And I was healthy. In my first pregnancy, I was living in Dublin and working for a Sunday paper there. I visited Calcutta to interview Mother Teresa and write about the street children, not knowing that the beginnings of my child lay curled up deep inside me like a prawn. I toured the sewers and the slag heaps and retched at the stench, which clung like shit to the back of my throat. I caught an infection, took anti-malaria tablets washed down with whisky. Amazingly, the baby emerged nine months later in one piece. My second pregnancy was much less eventful, no trans-global flights, no surprises, just a daily routine of work, pasta lunches and the wearing of sensible shoes. Over the years, I had undergone a physical renaissance and become an organic junkie. Even wine, my one remaining vice, has to be preservative-free. In preparation for Caoimhe's birth I didn't even take a paracetamol.

By twelve weeks the vague sickness that was our baby's calling card had gathered force and had taken over the running of my body like a finicky lodger. It didn't like porridge, bacon, cereal or fruit, it demanded litres of fizzy drinks at odd times which it quaffed and threw out with disgust. It called the tune on every single organ until my whole body was weary with trying to appease it. I'd lie down, only to find I was hungry; I'd eat, but it would only feed the nausea.

I started the day puking and I finished with a bedtime retch. In the beginning it was bearable because I thought by 14 weeks it would be gone. I counted them down. This week I couldn't stomach porridge, but by next week, who knows? A fried egg? And the next week would come and even dry toast would send me running to the bathroom. By 16 weeks I began to panic. At 20 weeks I felt resentful. At 24 weeks I was resigned to the fact I was one of those unlucky women in for the long haul, and at 28 weeks I quit work. I had been sick in my other pregnancies, but nothing like this. Later I discovered that mothers carrying babies with chromosomal abnormalities can be sick the entire length of the pregnancy. I'm glad I didn't know that then.

We did have a scan at nineteen weeks because I wanted to know the sex of the baby. We deliberated long and hard whether to find out; we had done so with the other two and this had somehow made me feel closer to them—they were no longer aliens with squatting rights, but living, breathing baby girls. I didn't really think there was anything wrong with this child.

She rumbled around my womb like low-grade thunder and every time the doctor measured my bump it had grown the required number of centimetres. At one stage, she was even on the large side. Still, I felt a little anxious on the day of the scan. Prenatal testing is a voyeuristic peek into a sacred, secret world and there was nervous trepidation about seeing her face for the first time, especially after having almost lost her. The doctor who performed the test raved about the new technology, which showed our baby pirouetting in the womb in glorious 3-D.

Conor thought she looked perfect, but when a close-up of her face loomed large on the screen, I couldn't help but exclaim, 'She looks like Spud on *Bob the Builder*.' She didn't look real. Like a work-in-progress, the features were there—I could see a nose, a mouth and two eyes, crudely set in an imperfect orb—but she looked about as human as a scarecrow. Anyway, the name stuck. From then on, my bump was known as Spud. We bought clothes for Spud, made plans for Spud. In my fantasies I saw her as a grown-up, red hair cascading down her back, long delicate fingers running up and down the piano with the effortless grace I have never acquired with all my years of practice. My daughters painted endless pictures of Spud: Spud on a horse, Spud going shopping, Spud in her pram. And as the due date got nearer, they'd ask: Will Spud come out today?

Spud needed a proper name. Conor, born and bred in Dundalk, was determined it would be Irish and we decided to call her Caoimhe, which means grace.

On Tuesday, June 17 at five o'clock in the afternoon, she finally gave the signal after a week of false starts. I can only wonder at the conversations which went on between her and my subconscious as to the right moment to drill her way out. I felt like we'd been in secret, sensitive negotiations the last few days, like foreign diplomats. I mused on what day of the week we would finally meet; I'm not superstitious by nature, but I secretly, stupidly, hoped it wouldn't be a Wednesday as I didn't want her to be 'full of woe'. Anyway, there I was, standing in a children's clothes shop buying a pair of lime green flares for my three-year-old daughter, Ceridwen, or Wynnie, as we tended to call her, when I was immobilised by a sharp pain which thrust upwards from my cervix and exploded into splinters across my pelvis. I went home and sat down at the piano. When I could no longer play, I decided, would be the time to go to hospital. I went through my repertoire: Mozart, Bach, and finally music from the film *Hans Christian Andersen*, when the chords evaporated in mid-air and I knew Caoimhe's excavation had really begun.

My first child was born after a 24-hour labour and an epidural. My second child was born after a 12-hour labour and a shot of pethidine. I wanted this birth to be drug-free. Perfect, because this was my last child and I wanted to get it right.

At 10 pm we headed for the local public hospital; by then the pains were arrestingly intense. I felt calm, drunk, happy, like I'd had a couple of glasses of rich, red wine and was at a party being eyed up by a good-looking stranger. The night felt electric with excitement and expectation; I had a warm, milky feeling that I was going to get lucky.

And then I arrived at the maternity wing, an unremarkable place of peachy walls and weary midwives who'd seen it all before. I was propelled into a room with a double bed, cupboards that hid the machines and implements of delivery, and a no-nonsense carpet. I was no longer a wild and sexy woman in my element, but a patient who needed monitoring, sorting out. Sit here, arm there, put this on, take this off. I'd come home from the party to find my disapproving mother waiting in the kitchen. I sat on the bed and the first tear slid down my cheek.

In anticipation of this awfulness, I had asked my friend Annabel to be at the birth, along with Conor. In many ways, Annabel is a photographic negative of me. While I am a devout atheist and cynic, she is a child of the New Age, a goddess-worshipper, who builds stone circles and gives her children unconventional names. Where my concerns often remain trapped in my head, hers are easily voiced. No way was she going to be bossed by a battleaxe in nursing uniform. She had given me her promise to 'roar like a lioness' on my behalf, thus allowing the primal, primitive part of my brain to take over during labour and birth unhindered, and so far she was living up to the pledge. Like a lawyer objecting to a jury member, she swiftly dispensed with the first midwife, who by coincidence had been at the birth of my second child, three and a half years earlier. (During that event she kept staring at her watch and yawning and I had hoped never to cast eyes on her again.) Her replacement was meek and quiet and manageable and took my refusal to have an internal examination with just a few concerned clucks and an acquiescent shrug.

I had fantasised and anguished about labour for so long, virtually since I knew I was pregnant. And now here I was, in the thick of it. Previously I had been swamped by the hugeness of it all, its ability to wash over me and bring me crashing down under the waves of the contractions, tossed and battered by panic. This time I could cope. The pain was confined to my uterus, and with each wave I was surfing the top of it, not drowning underneath. I was exquisitely, ecstatically alive and it felt wonderful.

And then suddenly it didn't. Suddenly it felt as if I was dying. I couldn't take any more; it was as if I had been flying through the air on a magic carpet and then looked down to discover there was nothing there. I remember the black terror. My waters hadn't even broken, I could only be two centimetres dilated and I'd reached my limit. I remember hearing Annabel's voice from far away saying, 'If you want this baby to be born on a Tuesday you'd better hurry up,' but I'd lost track of time and had no idea it was fifteen minutes to midnight. And then there was the most incredible sensation, like someone trying to turn my insides out. It rode through my lower body like a demonic two-headed beast; I couldn't stop it, the force of its sudden invasion overwhelmed me.

I'd catch my breath and it would come again: once, twice, three times; with each onslaught I was being pried apart. Soon I would be split open like a nut to reveal the tiny kernel. I was half standing, half kneeling, when Caoimhe's head emerged at seven minutes to midnight and then, oh joy, the warm wet slipperiness of her tiny body as it plopped onto the no-nonsense carpet.

My first startling memory of Caoimhe is that she was born within her amniotic sac, her face squashed up against the membrane like a doll wrapped in cellophane. Being born in the caul, I was told later, is believed to be a sign of good luck. The midwife peeled it back from her face and handed her to me, bits of grey jelly still clinging to her, like old glue.

She was beautiful. I think my first words were 'Where's your hair?' because my other two girls had emerged with a dark mop, but Caoimhe's head was lightly covered with soft fuzz, like a worn tennis ball.

The euphoria of her birth lasted only seconds before I was enveloped in a grey miasma. I don't know why because there was nothing about her appearance that rang immediate alarm bells. Wynnie had emerged red, wizened and as scrunched as an old tissue; by contrast, Caoimhe's planes were as smooth as a river pebble. It was her fingernails that troubled me, they were strangely arched like little tombstones. Her eyes were a bit different too; the closed lids were perfect semicircles framed with frilly lashes, giving her a look of the cartoon character Betty Boop. I thought she was really pretty. Still, I couldn't

shake off the anxious feeling. No one else seemed perturbed.
The obstetrician, who had rushed into the delivery room just
before Caoimhe's birth, weighed her and did the Apgar test, in
which she scored a satisfying eight. She did not appear floppy,
quite the opposite; she blindly thrust her limbs for the first
time into a vacuum of thin air.

At 7 pounds, 3 ounces, or 3¼ kilograms, she was smaller
than my second child, bigger than my first. So what was the
root of this anxiety? Did I subconsciously have an inkling of
her condition? Looking back, I think I must have had. The
near miscarriage early on had left a vapour trail of uncertainty throughout the pregnancy which had not
evaporated at birth. How else can I explain this lingering
solicitude? At the time, I put it down to shock; it had been
such a fast delivery. Her final descent took just six minutes—
faster than a pizza, was my rather lame joke. I went for a
shower and gave her to Annabel to hold. When I returned, she
and Caoimhe were asleep in the chair. Immediately I became
panicky and snatched the baby up. Was she still breathing? Of
course she was. Why was I so jumpy? I hadn't been like this
with the others. An hour later, we phoned Conor's parents in
Ireland. 'Who does she look like?' they wanted to know. I
looked at the heavily fringed Betty Boop eyes. 'No one in
particular,' I said. 'She looks like . . . Caoimhe.'

The nurses were keen to pack me off to bed. The hospital
was rotund in shape with each ward containing two beds built
around a central nurses' station. My bed was the farthest from
the door, next to the window. As the midwife busied herself
patting the pillows and arranging the perspex crib, she casually
inquired whether I'd had any prenatal testing. Perhaps I should
have clicked at that point, but, oddly, I didn't think this was a

strange question. It was two in the morning. I had just given birth, the baby seemed healthy and I was trying to understand my own panic, which, thankfully, was beginning to subside.

Annabel left, Conor left, the nurses left. I lay in the dark and watched the dusky shape of my new daughter next to me. She was intently observing her fingers, which were slowly uncurling in front of her face, like delicate strands of coral. It was at that point that I loved her. The anxiety lifted and I looked at her in delight and awe. 'We did it,' I whispered. The post-birth panic had been the shock of separation; for so long she had been as much a part of me as my heart, liver and lungs. And then she was gone, in six minutes she'd been brutally and sensationally torn from me. All that was left of our togetherness was her twisted stump and my deflated, empty belly. Now we were a cell divided. There was a foot between her bed and mine but it may as well have been a continent. I didn't know, after all, if I was prepared to let her go. I reached out and stroked her. Her opaque eyes stared blankly upwards; it was through her fingers, so singingly alive to touch, that our earliest communications were made.

I was just getting used to this moment: one, now two beings; our outrageous separateness being slowly healed in the dark, when the woman in the next bed started to snore. The night was rudely punctured by her rhythmic nasal roar, which would explode into a series of staccato movements every now and then, like a pig at the trough. I hated her with the fury of someone hormonally unbalanced.

My daughter was not unnerved by these crescendos, barely turning her head, whereas I restlessly changed positions, muttering under my breath, before finally falling into a fraught, frustrated sleep.

The next morning I awoke to the clatter of the tea trolley bringing breakfast in grey plastic Tupperware. Next to me Caoimhe slept: pink, fragrant and soft as marshmallow. I looked across at the baby in the next cot, purple as a bruised plum, and I felt smug.

A midwife came in to help me feed her, but the baby wasn't interested and she hadn't been the night before either. Put to the breast she fumbled and banged her head against my skin like one of those nodding dogs you see in the rear windows of cars. It hadn't particularly bothered me the previous night and I wasn't letting myself get alarmed now. I had discovered with my other two girls that breastfeeding—like the best of relationships—takes time to get established. This midwife also asked me about testing in pregnancy, but once again I failed to make a connection.

Why is this? I don't know. Perhaps I didn't want to know, was not ready to have my defences shattered. The obstetrician who delivered her came by and examined her slowly and carefully and remarked on her doll-like features, but nothing else. As she was leaving she said she would get the paediatrician to examine her, but once again I failed to pick up the thread. I thought this was routine.

Conor arrived with Ellie and Wynnie, nervously excited to be meeting their new sister. As we sat on the bed together, looking at this parcel which had plopped into their life, another midwife arrived at the scene, a midwife whose face remains seared on my brain, partly because she was perhaps the ugliest person I have ever come across, and partly because it was she who casually chucked the hand grenade into my well of postnatal bliss.

I can't even remember her name, but her face! It was

curiously ugly, like it had been wrenched inside out by someone in a bad mood.

I'd like to think my preoccupation with her appearance is not vindictive; I do believe the fact that her face is so vivid after all this time is as much to do with her ugliness as it is with the role she played in my life. After all, she was perfectly pleasant. She offered to take a photograph of us all. Wynnie hid behind the chair: she was struggling to manage her conflicting emotions, like a juggler who keeps dropping a ball. She was happy, cross, excited, bewildered and betrayed. Frustrated with her inability to handle such a load, she hid.

Eight-year-old Ellie, ever conscientious, was keen to get to school and so they left shortly after this awkward, impromptu photo session. I can hardly look at this snap-shot any more because it is too painful. It is the only one we have as the family of five we dreamt of being: me looking tired but serene; Conor, crazy-haired and manic, his smile a *risus sardonicus* through lack of sleep; Ellie pleased but self-conscious—she hates having her photo taken. Wynnie's leg protrudes from a chair and Caoimhe is just a sleeping, normal newborn, the only time in her life free of a label.

I remember I was sitting in the same chair where Wynnie had hidden when the ugly midwife came back to make my bed shortly afterwards. She, too, casually asked about testing in pregnancy and this time something sparked within my brain. 'Testing? Why do you ask?'

'It doesn't matter,' she replied without looking at me— concealing, rather than revealing, what she had to say.

I felt the first twinges of fear gathering momentum. 'Tell me, why do you ask?' I persisted, but she refused: 'It's not for me to say.' By now the fear was being swept along by anger at this game of cat and mouse. 'Tell me,' I said tersely, forcefully. She paused.

'We think your baby has a chromosomal abnormality,' and the carousel grinds to a halt.

'What sort of abnormality? What do you mean?'

'Down syndrome,' she says and I leave my body and levitate somewhere towards the ceiling. Heavy words, so lightly thrown, I think, oddly detached. I watch, from a space in the corner, as I look down at Caoimhe in my arms, and I see myself stroke her face. I hear my voice, surprisingly, say, 'I thought so.'

'The ears,' I say to the midwife, as I look at them, folded down at their tops. And then I was back in my body, demanding to see the obstetrician. I remember following the midwife out to the nurses' station and hearing her talking to the doctor on the phone—'She's asking questions'—and feeling awash with distrust. They had all known since Caoimhe's birth, but I hadn't allowed myself to know. The dishonesty was almost too much to bear.

The obstetrician came back. She was gentle but she couldn't look me in the eye. She was, she said, 60 to 80 per cent certain. She had her suspicions shortly after birth, by the appearance of Caoimhe's eyes and jaw, but she wasn't sure so she decided not to say anything. The paediatrician had done his rounds for the day, but he would be back the next day and would examine Caoimhe then. I was too shocked to be incredulous at this amazing disregard, but I did insist that she should be examined as soon as possible. A phone call was made and it was arranged for him to visit that evening at seven.

And then the midwife and the obstetrician melted awkwardly away and I was left to phone Conor, who had taken Wynnie out for a babycino and chocolate cake to celebrate. He returned to find my broken message that all was not well on the answering machine. A friend came to mind Wynnie and Conor returned to the hospital. 'Oh love,' was all he said, and kissed the top of my head, before picking up Caoimhe. I don't think at that point either of us felt any impulse to reject Caoimhe. I couldn't put her down. I held her close, possessively, defiantly. The three of us grimly clung to one another, braced like a rugby scrum against the rising tide of a future from which there was no escape.

Conor went home in the afternoon and arranged childcare so he could be present for the paediatrician's visit. But the doctor, a balding, elderly man in a herringbone jacket, turned up an hour early, and so once again I was forced to bear the news alone. He examined Caoimhe for five minutes before declaring he was 90 per cent certain the baby had Down syndrome and did I have any questions?

The rest of the week passed in a blur. The public hospital was a busy, bustling place but I felt suspended in time. Staff came and went, straightening sheets, collecting food trays, slipping in and out like shadows.

My grief and sadness and overwhelming sense of isolation felt so out of place in a maternity ward where happiness hangs like thick smog. In some ways it was harder for Conor. While I could allow myself the luxury of tears cocooned from the humdrum of everyday reality, he struggled to be stoic for the sake of our other two daughters. It was left to him to break the news to friends and family whose reactions were a diluted version of our own: shock, fear, sadness. No one knew whether to offer their congratulations or commiserations, and words, when they came, seemed forced and clumsy. On the second night, a new mother in the next bed held a party to celebrate the birth of her first child. As the champagne corks popped and the cameras flashed I stifled sobs into my pillow for the baby I hadn't had.

The cold cut of Caoimhe's diagnosis burst the honeymoon bubble that encompasses new parenthood. After all we had gone through in early pregnancy, this time we had really lost her. The dreams and fantasies I'd built over the past six months evaporated like cloud dust. Spud had vanished and a changeling placed in the crib. Every time I looked at her, I could no longer see her beauty, just her defects.

Conor and I were left alone to deal with the fallout of our dreams. On reflection, I find it ironic that couples agonising over whether to terminate a foetus with Down syndrome are offered counselling by trained professionals whereas we hardly got as much as a cup of tea. There was a general awkwardness among the staff when it came to talking about her diagnosis, or else it was ignored completely. Maybe I came across as a person who was coping, whereas inwardly I was flooded with the strangest sensations: grief, anger, disappointment, fear and an overwhelming love for this tiny creature who was still my child, and who was struggling with the very basic survival skill of sucking. Every moment was spent trying to get her to feed, but her low muscle tone, a characteristic of the syndrome, made it achingly difficult. I felt so helpless after each attempt left us both angry and confused.

As I sat with Caoimhe on my lap, stroking the muscles of her cheeks and throat in an attempt to stimulate a reflex, there were fleeting moments when I hated her for being different. I felt impatient with her for not being able to do something so basic, and terrified that this was going to be a pattern recreated all of her life.

How old would she be before she was toilet-trained? Would she ever be able to read or write? Hold a conversation? I wanted to know everything about Down syndrome but I was too terrified to find out. One of the nurses gave us a badly-printed handout from the Internet, but the words ran off the page and didn't make sense anyhow.

The day after the diagnosis, Caoimhe was taken away for a blood test, her heels cut with a razor and her blood squeezed onto a slide, so the extra chromosome could be examined through a microscope. I learnt that there are three types of Down syndrome; it was suspected she had standard trisomy 21, which is the most common. Basically it meant that in every cell of her body lurked an extra copy of the twenty-first chromosome, ready to cause potential damage. I could still manage a twisted smile to think of all the years I'd militantly refused to buy genetically-modified food and yet I'd given birth to a genetically-modified child.

But God, I felt so protective. One night I woke, hot and sweaty, to find Caoimhe gone from my side. I ran out to the nurses' station, heart thumping, calling for her. It turned out the paediatrician with the herringbone jacket had wanted to perform an echocardiogram to check for heart abnormalities, and since it was close to two in the morning, the nurses thought it best not to wake me. When I look back at this incident, small bubbles of anger continue to surface. Why wasn't I told? If Caoimhe had not had Down syndrome, would I have been? For me, there was a sinister ring of history to the event; in the past, people with intellectual disabilities were viewed as lesser citizens than the rest of us. Did they think Caoimhe wouldn't feel or notice my absence? And that I didn't want to be there?

The test was normal. I wasn't relieved as I hadn't been worried—at that point I was unaware that 40 per cent of babies with Down syndrome have heart problems. What did concern me was that Caoimhe's skin had acquired the yellowish tones of a fake suntan. She had developed jaundice and needed another blood test to check her bilirubin levels. This time Conor was determined to be with her, but the pathology nurses were reluctant. In another of those vignettes that has not lost its colour over time, I see Conor, polite but firm, and I see a nurse, small and brusque in her blue trousers and apron, trying to persuade him to wait with me. 'The baby will cry; it will be distressing,' she says, unable to recognise the absurdity of her argument. But Conor remains resolute and strokes Caoimhe's hair as they take a razor to her heel. His face is pale when he returns and she has aged a hundred years. The bud of her mouth is contorted into a rictus of shock and her skin a dull red from crying.

As the days passed in hospital, I continued to struggle with breastfeeding with little support. I remember feeling incensed when one of the midwives called my baby lazy. I knew nothing about Caoimhe's condition but I could see her gamely trying to latch on and I could feel her frustration when each attempt failed. In the end, formula milk was leached into her stomach via a gastric tube. I couldn't look.

There were blissful moments too. When the ward was quiet, when it was just us two, Conor and the girls having gone home, I could look down at Caoimhe and she was my beautiful baby with perfect skin and big dark eyes. It was like the two of us were encased in a safe warm bubble, but then thoughts of the future would barge into my mind like a gatecrasher at a party and the moment would be lost.

I could not equate this child with the image I had of Down syndrome. I had had very little contact with anyone who had the condition and the caricatures in my mind were locked in a time warp. I'd grown up in a small village in the north of England, and there had been a home for the mentally handicapped, as they were then called, on the periphery. I'd seen them there: badly-dressed, overweight men and women with pudding-bowl haircuts and trousers with elasticised waists. People who talked funny, people to be feared and avoided.

Nobody wants that for their child. I felt like the thirteenth fairy from 'Sleeping Beauty' had come along and cast a wicked spell. Down syndrome strikes at the heart of society's two most valued attributes: looks and intelligence. Needless to say I was ashamed of such thoughts. I'd worked hard to bury my prejudices and challenge stereotypes. Barbies were not encouraged in our house because I did not want my girls to grow up obsessed with their appearance. But look at me now! Crying because my daughter has a thick neck.

Four days passed in the hospital, with me struggling to contain my intense and ambivalent feelings, not to mention the incessant thoughts that ricocheted around my brain like boiling bubbles in a closed pan. I'd look at Caoimhe as she fumbled at my breast and in my mind's eye see her as an adult clumsily dropping her fork. Eventually we found our rhythm and the jaundice started to clear. On the fifth day we went home and we attempted to reconstruct family life from the wreckage of our crashed hopes.

Outside it had been raining and the world seemed a different place. Sharper, glassier somehow. In a state of grief you are painfully alive to sensation, like salt on a gash. Stepping into the house I could see it was exactly as I had left it less than a week ago; it bore all the hallmarks of familiarity but it belonged to another lifetime as if I were merely a visiting ghost. It was as if with Caoimhe's diagnosis I had undergone some sort of psychic death—with a creeping terror I realised that a part of me had gone forever along with the child who had been conceived in my bed and slept in my womb while I cleaned and painted these very walls.

In those first few days at home grief rendered me useless. I remain eternally grateful to friends who rallied round with their quiches, cooked dinners and bottles of wine, who'd take our children on outings to give us space without expecting anything in return. Conor and I are both private people who up until then had been crap at asking anyone for help, even each other. We felt gauche and awkward in the face of such kindness; our vulnerability made us cringe.

Slowly we began taking bigger forays into the world of Down syndrome, only to beat a hasty retreat when we inevitably bit off more than we could chew. We'd go to the local library and arm ourselves with books we were too afraid to read. The diseases and illnesses to which Caoimhe would be prone were listed with the emotional detachment of a shopping catalogue: heart problems, hearing problems, respiratory infection, leukaemia, blah blah. Like children watching a horror movie we'd peep through lattice fingers at the photos contained within the pages and then cover our eyes. I could only go so far before casting the books aside in favour of a Jilly Cooper blockbuster I'd also picked up to cushion the shock. How lovely it was at the end of the day to run away to Larkshire, where all the people were sleek and beautiful and all they cared about was humping each other.

One day shortly after arriving home, we found a large

orange envelope with a smiley face logo wedged inside the letterbox. At some point in the hospital Conor had summoned the courage to contact the local branch of the Down Syndrome Association. This was the information pack they had sent us and we opened it as if it contained a bomb. That evening in the sitting room we sifted through the contents with fascinated horror. The opening page showed a cartoon of what looked like an adult baby wearing a nappy and a large love heart and immediately I had to move on. Next came practical survival tips for the first few weeks and another cartoon baby bearing a close resemblance to Homer Simpson along with advice on how to bathe the 'little person'. I gave an involuntary shudder. What sort of a world had I entered?

Underneath the mess of brightly-coloured pamphlets spread out on the table I found an article entitled 'Welcome to Holland' by Emily Pearl Kingsley which described what it's like to discover your child has a disability. Kingsley likened it to planning a trip to Italy and getting all excited about seeing Rome's Colosseum, the statue of David and the gondolas of Venice, but when the plane lands you mysteriously find yourself in Holland. Here you must learn a whole new language and adjust your expectations accordingly. But, says the author brightly, Holland can be beautiful as well. There are windmills and tulips and Rembrandt. Maybe, but it wasn't like that for us. I felt as if we'd crash-landed in Disney World, a place of myths, make-believe and saccharine sentiment where everyone grins goofishly, is overweight and stupidly happy.

The rest of the pack was littered with information about how to make mobiles and how to dress the baby but I couldn't find the answers to my questions. What do I do if I hate my baby? Feel ashamed of her? How do I cope when people stare? As I drifted through the leaflets I could only conclude that such awkward emotional concerns were deliberately avoided.

Would my sadness ever leave? Probably not, I decided. But it would continue to be trammelled by a whole host of other feelings, not least, joy. Hopefully time, that great Band-Aid, would see emotions shake and settle like the flakes in a child's snow dome. I guess that's why I am writing this book, to make sense of the senseless, to create some order from the chaos in my head, so perhaps I can sleep at night.

A few weeks later I am looking down at my baby lying in my lap and all my fears are momentarily quashed, my prejudices melt away. She raises her hands and waves her fingers with all the grace of a Balinese dancer. They are beautiful fingers, long and tapered. Just right for playing the piano. We are back in our bubble, Caoimhe and I, and life is good. The feelings that wrap around my bones are blissful, they warm the very core of my existence. Beautiful girl, we are so lucky to have you. I am not yet in Holland, but I am tentatively beginning to challenge the misshapen beliefs and images left over from my childhood. This moment, and others like it, are patches of sunlight through tall dark trees. I don't know where Caoimhe might fit in society, but I know a family is a world in microcosm. And I know that right here, right now, she fits perfectly within my arms.

Chapter 2
Dispatches from the Shower

For those first few months after Caoimhe's birth, joy and grief had me in a tug of war. She was a beautiful baby, but she had a disability. When I was alone with her, when it was just us two, we were simply mother and child, a symbiotic organism locked in a rhythm as old as the moon. And then the memory of her diagnosis would loom up from nowhere and I would be consumed by fear, panic, sadness.

In times of crisis people often agonise over why such an event has happened to them. I don't recall asking 'why me'; I accepted my lot, but I was bloody angry that it was my turn, that my number had been called. I had done my time, I had limped through a difficult childhood and adolescence, but my twenties were the alchemy that turned alloy to gold. Jobs, boyfriends, opportunities rattled into place like pieces in a child's shape-sorter. And while I put it all down to good fortune, a quiet voice inside me believed you made your own luck. If I ate the right foods, worked hard, was a nice person, then I would reap the rewards. These simple measures would propel me safely through life. I had no control over the events that had pockmarked my childhood, but as an adult I was at the helm. And then came Caoimhe's birth and the tenets of my existence shattered like glass.

If we make our own luck, do we also make our own bad luck? When Caoimhe was a few months old I developed a sore throat after eating fish and was worried I'd swallowed a bone. The next morning I put her in the pram and walked to the nearest doctor's surgery. I was seen by a brisk red-faced woman with a booming voice who shone a torch down my throat but could find no bone. It looks like a mild virus, she said reassuringly, and I relaxed; I'd had a fishbone removed once before and it wasn't pleasant. I was on the verge of leaving, feeling buoyant with relief, when the GP peered down at Caoimhe kicking her bow legs happily and said 'Down's?' just like that. The entity of my daughter encapsulated in a short, sharp question as unexpected as a bullet.

'Yes,' I replied, stunned into compliancy. The GP asked my age and computed the stats in her head. 'Ah yes, a one in 350 chance. It's a lotto and you were unlucky.'

Was I? Walking home in a daze I thought back to those early months of pregnancy when we had almost lost her, and how lucky we felt at the 19-week scan when we saw her moving around my womb like a spaceman in a capsule. After my first daughter was born, I had developed an autoimmune disease of the thyroid gland. The doctor who was treating me told me I was lucky. If I was going to have an autoimmune disease, this was the one to have. After Caoimhe was born, a friend who is also a GP said I was lucky. If I was going to have a child with a disability, Down's was the one to have. Luck is clearly a matter of perception. How ironic that the four-leaf clover, one of nature's more agreeable mistakes, has come to represent it.

I didn't feel unlucky but I did feel tarred. A mother and baby is an interdependent entity; one does not exist without

the other. It was as if I, too, carried Caoimhe's stigma. When
I took her out, I could feel people staring at her, this blighted
product of my womb, and I felt like I'd failed as an upstand-
ing member of society. All around me were mothers with
chubby, healthy babies, and pregnant women with bellies full
of promise. And although they smiled at us when they passed
by in the street, I sensed their pity, a wasted emotion that only
made me feel more isolated. It was the elderly, with their
habit of peering into prams, whom I dreaded meeting
the most. If ever I was standing in a queue I'd nervously scan
the immediate vicinity for preying grannies; in my mind's eye
I'd see one closing in, weathered face wreathed in smiles then
buckling in shock as realisation dawned and a cracked voice
exclaimed: 'Oh! A mongol!' Whenever anyone came close to
Caoimhe the palpable mass of protectiveness that sits heavy
at the bottom of my stomach would lurch and I'd look down
at her pale little face with its slanting, enchanting eyes and
feel shaky with love.

Caoimhe's birth had aligned me to a new group of
individuals, those touched by grief. People seemed different,
but of course it was me who had changed. I no longer had
time for superficial friendships, I could only connect to the
raw stuff that makes us human. A friend in Ireland sent me,
by e-mail, an outpouring of her domestic sorrows and then
asked whether I was sick of whingers—but my answer was
No! I loved them. I got perverse pleasure from other people's
miseries. One evening a friend who had split with her boyfriend came around to rake over the ashes of their dead
relationship. We sat until midnight picking at the knots in the
ties that could no longer bind, a fruitless, repetitive exercise,
soothing as balm. She doesn't know it, but I got far more from

that night than she did. Other people's problems were solvable—but not mine. Down syndrome has no get-out clause; it is not a condition limited to a limb that can be replaced, or an organ that can be removed—the extra chromosome and its genetic overload will vibrate through every cell of Caoimhe's being till death. There are no miracle cures, heartfelt appeals, no desperate flights to specialists, no pursuit of distraction at all, just an endless plain of childhood, chronic catarrh and a slow decline into dementia. I realised early on that the hard struggle of acceptance offered the only real chance of happiness.

But how? Grief keens the senses like steel blades and every sensation felt like sun on raw skin. Stripped of my defences, I saw the world with naked eyes. Habitual routes I pounded day after day to ease the pain contained trees and walls and cracks and graffiti that I'd never noticed before and I wondered where I'd been all this time. Familiar objects were echoes from the old world, a place of safety and predictability, where shocking things happened to other people. I'd see men and women wearing their self-assuredness like armour and I'd marvel at a naivety which had been mine until a week ago. Like me, they did not know that such indelibility was no more than an illusion. I wanted to rush up to them and tell them that pride comes before a fall; it would only take a phone call, a careless mistake, a wrong step for their chain mail to float away like confetti, leaving them soft and raw and bleeding.

Misery scorns happiness and leaves us marooned.

I would look at perfect children and almost wish for something to go wrong, so that I would have someone else to inhabit my island. Fortuitously, as a counterpoint to all of this melancholy, my sense of fun was also heightened. I developed an appreciation for frivolity that had previously been in short supply. A couple of weeks after Caoimhe was born, I stole an hour while she was sleeping to make my annual pilgrimage to the hairdressers. Here I was given, as always, a tasteless cup of tea in a fashionable but unserviceable stainless steel cup and a fondant chocolate wrapped in silver foil, bearing the company's crest. Previously I'd felt irritated at such egotistical indulgence, such ridiculous vanity, but not this time. In a world where shocking things happen, I was grateful that someone had taken the trouble to restore the balance with such trivial minutiae.

I dreaded breaking the news to friends and family. As most of them lived in England or Ireland it was often done by phone over the ensuing weeks. I worked on keeping my voice even as I delivered the punchline—It's a girl and she has Down syndrome—relieved that they couldn't see the agony in my face. I am not good at showing emotion; to do so leaves me vulnerable and open to imaginary attack. I found that people did not know how to react to Caoimhe's birth, uncertain whether to offer their congratulations or commiserations; some did the first, some the latter, and the more sensitive did both. Some well-meaning person sent me a eulogy from someone's funeral which she thought would be appreciated, but I'd just given birth! This is life, goddammit. Not life as we know it, but life all the same.

We lost count of the number of comments about children with Down syndrome being 'happy'. We received this old cliché with the same damp enthusiasm as a consolation prize on school sports day. No parent wants their child relegated to a homogeneous group of happy half-wits, without person-alities of their own. What was worse than these tactless, though well-meaning, remarks were those friends who said nothing. When Caoimhe was six weeks old, and the ache of grief still stiff in my bones, I slowly and painfully began to circulate. One of those early outings was to a birthday party where her diagnosis was never mentioned. People came over to chat politely and then flittered away like butterflies in search of something brighter, tastier. I met a woman from my birthing classes whose baby had been born a few weeks before Caoimhe. Our chatter was formal and awkward, like foreigners handicapped by different mother tongues. We regaled each other with our stories of labour, both of us grasping at shared experiences of normality whilst farcically ignoring the screaming obvious. And when the moment of escape came, by way of her baby's squawks of hunger, we both smiled at one another, relieved to be rid of the burden of pretence.

What do you say to a mother in a bipolar state of joy and grief? In cases of stillbirth, there is the solid indisputable evidence of a body: lifeless, but real. We can express our compassion, our sorrow, even the most awkward among us can mumble our condolences and move hurriedly on. But when the baby is born alive, albeit disabled, there is confusion; many of my friends were willing to share in my delight but skirted shyly around my grief for the baby I hadn't had. I don't know whether it was lack of understanding or the insidious virus of political correctness that stilled their tongues. Perhaps they were frightened of saying the wrong thing, but silence was worse.

When Caoimhe was a few months old we arranged to meet several families we had known for some years at an open-air symphony concert in a suburban park. It was typical Melbourne weather: the day had started hot and bright but by the time the orchestra was due to start, the air was melancholy and fat with rain. While the children played together at the front of the stage, holding out their hands to catch the first spillage from the clouds, we hunkered down on damp tartan rugs and busied ourselves with our picnics. Next to us, Caoimhe lay in her pram, her starfish hands making fists at the trees. And then came the slow sinking realisation: we were being ignored. One of the couples, pregnant with their second child, was deliberately avoiding us. Conor and I held a low, brief tactics meeting and a plan was speedily conceived. He would mind Caoimhe while I steeled myself to approach the female, un-encumbered by the blight of my daughter. This I did. Conversation was bright and artificial and revolved around her pregnancy. Not once did she ask after my baby. I tried to bear in mind that she may have had fears about her own pregnancy, but it still hurt. I returned from my reconnaissance mission, wounded and seething. At the interval, Conor, armed with Satan's spawn herself, attempted to engage with both of them, but while they were able to talk vacuously about the weather, work and the orchestral ensemble, they didn't even glance at Caoimhe resting on Conor's hip, mouth opening and closing like a ventriloquist's dummy. On the drive home, Conor's knuckles were white with anger and Caoimhe screamed uncharacteristically. Did she know, I wondered, that there were people out there who would rather she wasn't around? Who found her too confronting to be in her presence? When I got home I cried buckets for all the averted gazes she was yet to meet, for the blank stares she will puzzle over, for the sniggers and whispers that will confuse and hurt her.

These unpleasant, though thankfully isolated, encounters shook me deeply. Only in our immediate circle of close

friends where Caoimhe was accepted without question could
I feel safe. Venturing outside the confines of their security
compound required me to psyche myself up. Like an army
major I would go through the drill: thoughtless comments,
sideways stares spoke volumes about them, not us. They have
the problem, I would tell myself over and over like a mantra.
But the truth is, I didn't believe it. Pedestrians would pass me
by, we were forgotten in an instant, but their looks and stares
and comments about 'Down's babies being lovable' would
stick like tar. And I'd go home and work hard to mentally
scrub them off.

Why are we so uncomfortable in the presence of disability?
Perhaps because it reminds us of our own destructibility, and
because of this we don't want to acknowledge its existence,
despite the statistics which will tell you that 10 per cent of the
population has some form of handicap. But in a world where
perfection matters, people with differences are like ghosts:
they are all around us but can only be seen by a few. Disability
is society's blind spot, and now that the scales have fallen
from my eyes, I can see its injustices everywhere. Like a sinner
who turns to God I became quite evangelical in my deter-
mination to alter the status quo. One of the answers, I
decided, was for people with disabilities to become more
visible. I scoured the media for photos of babies with Down
syndrome but there were virtually none. Ethnic children are
well represented in texts of baby management, cookbooks
show cheerful jelly babies waving spoons, but the disabled
child simply doesn't exist. I scoured over one hundred back
copies of *Hello!* magazine where celebrity mothers were more
concerned with their post-partum diet than their babies
which lay draped like expensive decorations on cream couches

without so much as a cleft palate or a club foot. The exception
to this was Katie Price (A.K.A. Jordan), with her son, Harvey; I
find myself unexpectedly allied to her. My response was to
dress Caoimhe in vibrant clashing colours. Forget dusky
pinks and pastels, my child was going to be seen.

———

Her wardrobe was a welcome diversion from the reality of
life, which in those early weeks was too often fraught and
grim. Caoimhe was over seven pounds at birth but was slowly
and steadily failing to thrive. Each week her recorded weight
slid off the charts like melted ice cream. I read in some baby
manual that it's supposed to be impossible to overfeed a
breastfed baby, but Jesus, I tried. When I wasn't pouring milk
into her hungry red mouth, I was attached, bovine-style, to a
pump, expressing it into a bottle. Her lips pinned me like a
dead butterfly but it made no difference. After every feed the
milk would come right out again in a forceful arc. Messy, wet,
sloppy, sticky, it would spill on clothes and cushions and
pillows and eventually dry before I could get to it, leaving a
fine coating like a salt pan.

I tried not to take it personally but after all the effort to get
the milk down her in the first place, it seemed like a rude
gesture of defiance. Often she would fuss at the breast and cry
and pull away like I was poisoning her. And we would go
through the same routine day after Groundhog-style day.

———

I laughed hollowly at the death of the control-freak, my former persona. Before the birth I had stuck labels in all the cupboards in a vain attempt to get the family to put things away. I cleaned and scrubbed and pounded the house into some sort of order, but in the space of a few weeks Caoimhe was single-handedly responsible for turning my citadel of calm into chaos. My hair became matted because I never seemed to find time to brush it. I became thinner as she sucked and spewed the weight off me. Sometimes I would see myself in the mirror and catch my breath. My face wore the appearance of a garden gone to seed: my skin was red, my eyebrows had strayed from their allotments and my wild hair was falling out in handfuls. I recently read a newspaper article about how mothers of children with disabilities age more quickly than others: apparently chronic stress causes the body to break down faster at a molecular level. I had never really appreciated my looks until they were about to vanish.

I was, of course, more concerned with Caoimhe's weight than my wrecked visage. We needed medical help, so we took her to a paediatrician who called her Pussycat and examined her gently. 'She is borderline malnourished,' was his alarming diagnosis. He wanted to x-ray her gut for webbing in her duodenum which may have been preventing the milk from being properly absorbed, a problem, he said, which is more likely in babies with Down's. I did not want her to be x-rayed. She was hardly two months old. Could it be my diet that was affecting the milk, I asked, and he looked at me with the patient condescension that doctors reserve for new mothers. 'There's an elephant sitting in the road,' was his Zen-like answer, meaning, I suspect, that this was an obstacle we had to clear first. So we took her to the hospital and I'll never forget her propped up on the bed, head on one side because her neck muscles were still not quite strong enough to hold it straight, wearing a starched white nightgown. When she smiled at the two nurses holding her hands she looked like a lopsided angel. Above her towered the giant metal x-ray machine.

——

Conor and I, in the same room, wore heavy lead aprons to deflect any stray rays, and I felt sick at the idea of Caoimhe's tiny frail body being subjected to such a silent bombardment. She was given a bottle of barium meal to drink, a chalky white substance spiked with sugar, which she took uncomplainingly. The x-ray machine tracked it as it travelled down her throat and into her gut, like sand through the narrow neck of an egg timer.

There was nothing wrong with her structurally, but her body remained a deflated balloon. By now the baby-health nurse was visiting every other day to weigh her and I dreaded those visits. One night as I stripped her for her bath, that ever-present knot of anxiety did a double twist; she looked like a little scrap of tinned salmon, a bony chain of spine poking through her pink flesh. I couldn't bear to look.

Up until then, the wisdom of instinct had deferred to the expertise of science, but now it was time to trust my buried intuition. Four years earlier my eldest daughter, Eleanor, had been diagnosed with coeliac disease, a hereditary genetic condition characterised by intolerance to gluten. I had been told there is no real evidence to show that gluten gets into breast milk, but I removed it from my diet anyway, along with dairy products. Within 24 hours Caoimhe's vomiting had stopped along with her explosive bowel movements and frothy green nappies. From that point on, her weight steadily began to climb.

With the feeding under control we had more time to worry about the relentless round of appointments which crowded our calendar in those early days like a debutante's dance card. Eye tests, hearing tests, blood tests, more hearing tests—I became over-familiar with the tatty interior of Melbourne's Royal Children's Hospital, a 40-minute drive from our house. For Caoimhe's first hearing test, her threadbare scalp was scrubbed with an exfoliant to roughen the surface so the electrodes would attach better. It made her cry. My role, as the evil assistant, was to nurse her into a sleep-like state. Tiny sounds were fed into her ear and the part of her brain activated by noise was monitored by EEG. We watched silently as wavy peaks and troughs drifted across the screen, revealing what I had suspected all along—that her hearing was perfect. But, of course, I was only her mother, a job diluted by the team of experts who had squeezed into my life since her diagnosis.

———

After the test I went to the loo and was furious that there was no toilet roll to the point that my eyes stung with tears. You don't have to be a psychologist to know they were nothing to do with the lack of loo paper. I don't like hospitals; they only remind me how fragile we are. Children's hospitals, where the ordinary miracle and tragedy of life and death are mercilessly intertwined, are a particularly confronting place for parents.

We were lucky. Time after time, the tests revealed nothing. No problems with hearing or vision, no thyroid problems, bowel obstructions, heart problems, no leukaemia. The more specialists we saw, the more my daughter shrank from me until she was merely an object being scrutinised by quality control. Children with Down syndrome, it seems, are prone to virtually every disease and condition imaginable. The various medics we saw would reel off a litany of disasters awaiting Caoimhe. In their eyes, she was a time bomb of ill health ticking closer to explosion. I was alarmed, and anguished about bombarding her fledgling immune system with the standard childhood vaccines made of sinister-sounding ingredients. We were met with shocked disapproval when we declared our intention not to have her vaccinated at such an early age.

Finally, I took her across the other side of the city to a doctor from Latin America, who was trained in anthro-posophical medicine, which is based on the spiritual and mystical teachings of the Austrian philosopher Rudolf Steiner, for his advice. The doctor was a small dark man who moved quietly and spoke with an accent thick and gluggy as soup. Through the window of his cluttered consulting room I could see parrots on the lawn. He listened to the torrid history of Caoimhe's short life, nodding thoughtfully. I felt he was the first medic who saw her as an individual instead of a moving chromosomal error. After a slow and gentle examination, he declared her immune system healthy and strong. We felt more confident about our decision to delay the vaccinations.

Stress wound itself around me like a python in those early days. There were times when I couldn't breathe; I'd lie in bed at night feeling crushed by the day that had mercifully passed.

And the next day I'd get up and do it all over again: the appointments, the cooking, the feeding, the grieving.

Physically, it was like lumbering around under water. My arms and legs met with resistance every time they moved. My head felt full of cul-de-sacs. A thought would start, would be re-routed and eventually get lost in my brain's suburban wilderness. My hands and voice moved out of sync like a marionette's. I feared making some dreadful social faux pax, like being caught in the supermarket wearing a shower cap. Once I drove off to a school function in my carpet slippers, but fortunately Ellie discovered my error before we got to the venue and I was able to go home and change.

I tried so hard to appear normal for the sake of the other two, I was weary with the effort. I felt I was under the searching gaze of their spotlight and must perform accordingly. If I could cope, so could they. My only refuge was the shower, a two-foot-square Perspex sanctuary, where I could think and breathe and cry. Sometimes it was like stepping into Dr Who's Tardis: I'd turn on the taps, close my eyes and mentally press the rewind button, travelling back in time to periods of my life when I was not weighed down by the ball and chain of Caoimhe's disability.

I'd be 24, living in a semi in London, sw4, earning good money working for a national newspaper, watering myself regularly with champagne. Remember that time I got half an inch too much chopped off my hair and I hid in my room and cried? Ha! Remember the panic when I couldn't decide what to wear for Simon's party and the taxi would be rocking up in 10 minutes? The white Ghost number or the Jigsaw dress? Will it be takeaway pizza tonight, or shall I have Indian? Decisions, decisions. And all ahead of me was the burden of my inescapable future, travelling towards me, slowly but steadily, ready to hit me right between my unseeing eyes.

Fast forward 12 months, and I am backpacking around the world. I have tramped through South East Asia, Australia and New Zealand and now I am on the final leg of my journey: India. I have landed in Delhi, it is dusk and I am trudging around the Janpath district, where cheap, over-flowing guest-houses are scattered like an oozing rash, looking for somewhere to stay. This is my first visit to India and I am blown away by the anarchy of the place: the children with grimy unwiped bottoms who shit in the gutter; the adults who continually hawk and spit great globules of mucus onto the unmade street—I feel I have touched down in the world's largest public toilet. And in the middle of it all sit the cows: placid, patient, adored.

Thankfully I have a companion to buffer the shock, a tall thin Australian boy called Alon, whom I have just met at the airport. We take it in turns to check out the guesthouses but everywhere appears full. Apparently there has been a riot in another part of the city, and travellers have flocked to Janpath for safety. There is nowhere. We decide to try the old part of the city and hail an auto-rickshaw. The driver sees us coming. He knows a place for us to stay: nice hotel, special price, and he will take us. I am not so tired not to know that I am about to be ripped off, but too weary to care. So we go and lo, there is one double room left; it's something like $40 but we take it anyway because by now it is past midnight. I climb into my sleeping bag on top of the shiny crimson bedspread, but Alon cannot sleep. He opens a long thin cotton bag and pulls out a didgeridoo. It is two in the morning but Alon feels he must play it. He sits cross-legged on the red satin and from the didgeridoo comes a deep mournful lowing, a sound not dissimilar, I imagine, to a sacred cow being hit by a motorised rickshaw. So here we have a bizarre situation: me sharing a double bed with a total stranger who is playing a didgeridoo. Alone with Alon this tableau seems fraught with the possibility of danger and there are several thrilling conclusions: Alon and I are seduced by the magic of India and become lovers—not likely!; Alon turns out to be a thief and steals all my travellers cheques; or worse, he is actually a murdering psychopath luring young women to a premature end with his lovable hippy persona.

In truth, travelling sharpens the senses and I am not the person I was when I started out from London six months ago. Stripped of the props of Western living I have discovered what I lost as a child: my visceral self. I believe Alon to be harmless. He has come to India to find a guru and learn to be a healer. I fall asleep as he describes his meditation techniques.

In the morning we head towards the Paharganj district, a noisy predatory marketplace close to the railway station with laneways full of cheap guesthouses. It's absolutely packed, there are stalls selling anything from dishmops to dhal, and cars and cows are everywhere. I need to escape the shrill decibels of Delhi; in three weeks time I am meeting my boyfriend of five years in Mumbai, and my plan is to travel across Rajasthan as far as I can in that time, and then fly the rest of the way. I go to tourist information and try to arrange trains, buses and flights, but the two men at the desk are nefarious and unhelpful. With smiling white teeth framed by identical black moustaches they ask me my star sign.

After two frustrating hours peppered with plenty of peacock preening and cringe-worthy moments, I depart with some sort of itinerary.

I think a lot about those first few weeks in India while I am in the shower, perhaps because the feelings I experienced there were so confronting, so stark, so unprocessed. I remember seeing for the first time the cold majesty of the Taj Mahal, rearing up from the hot dusty plains littered with the carcasses of cows, and a lump forming in my throat at the tragic beauty of such a monument. The story goes that the emperor Shah Jahan built it as a magnificent gesture of love for his wife, Mumtaz Mahal, who died as their fourteenth child was being born. At that time I had no understanding of the mechanics of childbirth, the thrill of risk that occurs when life and death dance so close, but at dusk I would watch the sun sink behind the white minarets, and the air still felt pungent with the prince's sadness even after three centuries. I remember the faded watercolour beauty of the city of Udaipur; the red London buses in Mumbai; the sacred lake at Pushkar scattered with pink and yellow petals. None of these moments came cheaply. To get to these places I zigzagged across Rajasthan on buses and trains, often sleeping chained to my rucksack, watched silently by scores of dark, staring eyes. On one bus journey I awoke to find an unwelcome hand creeping up my thigh; on another, across a narrow jagged mountain road, I was unnerved to discover the driver was high on pot.

From a continual backdrop of frustration and confusion came moments of absolute clarity, pure as raindrops. It was as if in these split moments I gained knowledge which was not at the time understood. I was subconsciously collecting it, like scraps, for the future.

The epochal event of the trip was meeting my boyfriend in Mumbai. He had flown there unaware that during our six-month separation I had become love's leaking vessel; my feelings had slowly and steadily trickled away. And now, as I saw him waving cheerfully across the arrivals hall, I was filled with love's vanquishers: doubt, silence, loneliness. This was my first taste of proper grief, bitter as unripened fruit. We held hands as we walked the busy streets, but his clasp, once as familiar as old slippers, now felt awkward and odd. Those three weeks with him were agony for both of us. On the last night we lay in bed at some cheap rundown hotel in Goa after a valedictory dinner, crying silent tears for what could have been but had gone forever. Our future together was as untenable as our separation had seemed just months earlier. I don't know what had gone wrong, other than to say that during my travels I had split and shed several skins, and in doing so discovered parts of me I never knew existed but could not co-exist with him.

In many ways, India was the boot camp for Caoimhe's birth. There were plenty of moments in my day when I was high on love, others when life was a battle for survival in uncharted territory. Fear stole my words and I would retreat, mute, to the attic in my head, staring out at the world through tearless eyes. Sometimes I'd look at her and catch my breath, seeing only the features which set her apart from her sisters, and I was filled with a primal need to destroy. In my mind I straightened her eyes, sculpted the flat back of her head into a perfect sphere, wrung her neck gently until it thinned and lengthened in my coaxing hands like wet clay. I felt angry with her for having Down's, angry at the world for dealing her this affliction. It was best when she was sleeping, when her eyes were closed and she couldn't see the guilt of my ambivalence; she was still and perfect and my love was pure, untrammelled by any interference.

During the day, Conor and I moved like a pantomime horse, devastated as individuals, but together we could just about get by. If one of us was absent it was like a missing limb. When Caoimhe was about six weeks old, Conor tried to re-establish his working life as a PhD student, but with both our extended families abroad it was too difficult. Both our careers, which up until this point had given our lives definition, were impatiently pushed aside like children's colouring books.

With no family around, we needed help but we didn't know where to get it. We phoned the local council and they sent around a woman with a clipboard. We offered her tea; she offered us sympathy but not much else. The best she could do for us was to arrange some respite care, but at that stage Caoimhe was welded to my nipple, so that wasn't going to be of any use. All we wanted was someone to do the housework or cook a meal once in a while. The woman nodded her petrified helmet of beige hair as she listened to our lament and then said, bizarrely, 'I can really understand why people abuse their children.' I figured this was my cue to confess: 'Oh yes, we beat our children senseless with the stress of it all.' In which case, it seems, we would have got help. Families considered 'at risk' have priority. But our children must watch their parents deal with their grief, cook dinner, do the washing, take the baby to endless rounds of appointments, make their lunch, take them to school and just be bloody grateful that they don't physically bear the brunt.

Then, among the drift of leaflets on disability services which didn't seem to apply to us, we found a small, modest fridge magnet with a magic number, a hotline to heaven. It was a 24-hour care line offering practical support when you needed it. Anonymous, faceless—I had no idea who ran it, or who funded it, all I knew was that when I rang it, a calm voice would say: 'Tell us what you need.' No forms, no clipboards, no assessments. Just help. Hoovers, dusters, capable women in rubber gloves, who flicked around the grime of my house, no questions asked, or eyebrows raised. I stuck the fridge magnet firmly and squarely in the middle of our fridge, next to the one advertising mother's other little helper, Nando's Chicken takeaway.

It's not that there wasn't help available—over the coming months, when we had more energy to go digging, we unearthed charities and support groups. What was missing in those raw, unwashed days was a wise, efficient person who could point us in the right direction, give us the numbers, tell us where to look.

Our problem was that we had no family on hand to stuff the gaps. I'd look at my Persil-bright, coping friends with their mothers and mothers-in-law and aunties round the corner and plot a kidnap. Surely just one little granny, one unassuming aunt wouldn't be missed in these large extended families.

I wished I could be transported back to Ireland. I'd get into the shower and imagine it taking off and when it landed I'd step out to the smell of a Sunday roast which someone else had cooked. There'd be a soft rain falling and a fire in the grate. There would be pubs with dark cloistered recesses where I could sit anonymously in the gloom. The sky would be lined with protective woolly cloud. Day after day I'd stand under the jet of hot water and run away from the Lucky Country with its shrivelling exposed heat and rigid hierarchy of care.

Australia, a country we had come to nine years earlier in search of freedom, had turned into our captor. Here we were, marooned on a barren brown landmass slowly floating into oblivion. My waking moments were consumed with plans of escape, but our non-existent finances made it impossible. At the time, Conor was on a modest scholarship and I was on unpaid maternity leave; we could hardly afford a concession train fare down the coast, let alone shift the contents of our entire life halfway across the world. I felt trapped.

——

The irony is that we had always planned to go back, ever since we arrived one grey wet day in February, me four-and-a-half months pregnant with our first child, and not even a knife and fork to our name. At the time we believed we were looking for adventure, a last flirtation with youth before we entered the practical world of parenting. What crap! Only as time passed did I see that we were not romantically seeking adventure at all, but running away from the reality of an unplanned pregnancy. We had fled, our smiling exteriors masking our grief for a life that had halted as abruptly as a train crash, a life that our friends continued to flaunt—of parties, pubs and late-night drinking, smoky bars and taxi queues, spontaneity and getting up at noon. Only months earlier, I had ached for a baby I thought I'd never have; now it had been thrust upon me unexpectedly. One part of me was delighted, ecstatic, but another railed against the shock of it all. I had wanted to set my house in order first, to be mentally prepared for such an important guest; instead, the foetus had landed in a building site. Motherhood, with its girded underwear and sensible shoes, seemed anathema to me. I was not ready to become fat and egg-shaped in front of my svelte, successful friends; the thought of being relegated to the dumping ground of maternity as my old self melted absolutely horrified me. The child sleeping deep inside me had unknowingly smashed my carefully-constructed image, my armour against myself. We left because we felt we no longer belonged.

We were an unlikely couple in many ways. At the time, Conor, sensible and down-to-earth, was an engineer making microchips, and I was working for a Sunday newspaper in Dublin, where I had drifted after being unable to settle back in London after my travels. We were introduced by a mutual male friend I had met in New Zealand and had formed an unromantic friendship. Conor wore slippers and was nice to my dog and I liked that. One night, at a New Year's Eve ball in Galway, he kissed me and to my surprise I found myself responding. By the next weekend he'd virtually moved in.

When I told Conor nine months after that first kiss that he was going to be a dad, he scratched his head and stared silently at the carpet. We went to the local pub and had a pint of Guinness and I lit a cigarette, and there was an air of mourning to the occasion because I knew that this was going to be the end to my smoking. I still remember my last cigarette, pulling on it roughly, the pleasure of inhaling tainted by the knowledge that the tiny embryo was choking.

On a January day we left Dublin, the nascent bump of our daughter submerged under my Donegal sweater, and came to Melbourne—just for two years, we told Conor's parents, to buffer the wrench of our leaving. Five months later I gave birth to our first daughter at a large, busy, city hospital, and it was one of the loneliest experiences of my life. Conor would go off to work and I would sit playing with my child in our unheated Melbourne flat, knowing no one, waiting for him to come home. And then slowly, unrecognisably, things started to get better. I got a job as a journalist on the local paper and felt something of my old shattered self return. We made friends, money, and connections and had another baby. We still planned to go home . . . one day. Australia was no longer a terrible mistake that we refused to admit, but we were still too unsettled to call it home. We stood with our feet straddling the equator.

And then came Caoimhe and the question of returning became constant and urgent. Our future was no longer a speck on the horizon, but loomed large and threatening in our faces. Who would look after her when we were gone? What family did she have in Australia, apart from her sisters? And was it fair that they should spend their lives unable to stray from the radius of her shadow, guarding her like two stone lions, rooted and still? In Ireland there would be cousins, uncles, aunts, grandparents who could love her and watch out for her. Six months after Caoimhe's birth, Conor's brother and his wife had a daughter. The pain of envy that sat in the pit of my stomach at the news of their healthy baby was tempered by the hope that she may be another ally for Caoimhe.

In the shower I'd make mad plans; I'd have another baby! And another! I'd devote my life to viviparity, churning out children like a bloody cement mixer if it meant that she would never feel lonely, because that was the worry that embedded in me like a splinter. I'd see her as a grown-up, overweight and fumbling as she counted her money to buy an ice cream; I'd see her on a bus being laughed at by a bunch of kids; I'd see her crying tears of frustration at being misunderstood, her thoughts held hostage by poor speech. I saw happy images too, poignant ones: Caoimhe slowly walking down the aisle on her wedding day with a smile on her face like a gash in an apple.

When I emerged red raw from the sting of the shower I'd throw myself with abandon into the moshpit of motherhood. I'd sing with a shrill jolly voice, blow raspberries that were a little too forceful, rick my mouth into an unnatural smile. I had some desperate need for Caoimhe to enjoy these early months because I felt they would protect her from the inevitable sadness that was to come. In the playground, on the bus, she could wrap her babyhood around herself like a cloak and bury her nose in its warmth, returning to a time in her life when she was blissfully ignorant of her difference, when she was the same as everybody else, the equal of the blond-haired blue-eyed baby who smiled at her across the room.

Each day as she lengthens and uncurls I am singingly aware of my role in her life: her dependence, her future, sits heavily on my shoulders. This is what it means to be a grown-up and it's scary. Beautiful girl, I am helpless with love, I feel as if my whole life has been preparing for your arrival. And now you are here and I stare at you, mysterious, foreign and fragile as an egg, and it is my turn to scratch my head and fumble because I don't know what to do.

Chapter 3
Owner Manual

The story of my life with Caoimhe began with fear. Only the first nine hours of her existence remain untainted. Over the ensuing months the fear changed in size and intensity like the sun's shadow, and although there have been times when it shrinks to virtually nothing, I doubt it will ever truly disappear.

Where does it come from? In those early days I would look down at her and see a beautiful baby, delicate as a bubble, and I would be filled with a pristine love. But fear has no time for the present; it lurks among the dark shapes and alleyways of the future. And there was plenty out there to foster it.

I learnt early on that fear wears an impersonal face. Only minutes after her diagnosis, the doctor who'd delivered Caoimhe, who had measured the hill of my bump over changing seasons while chatting about football practice and muddy boots, her presence warm and comforting as mashed potato, was talking awkwardly about Caoimhe's 'intellectual deficit'.

The thin prelude of my daughter's life was marred by tests: echocardiograms on her heart; heels poked and prodded and squeezed for droplets of reluctant blood; bald head scrubbed and electrodes attached. The violence of it all appalled me. The printed fact sheets given to me by a nurse in the hospital shortly after the attack of her diagnosis laid out the stark chronology of her future: numerous respiratory infections in childhood and an increased risk of leukaemia; hearing and sight problems; thyroid malfunction and an early death at around fifty-five. The perfect shell of her newborn body would soon split and crack as she grew awkwardly, clumsily, revealing an underdeveloped nasal bone, a large tongue, small genitalia, mottled skin and short arms and legs. At the back of the handout was a list of diagnostic tests I could have in future pregnancies, and I felt humiliated, chastised. The black-and-white diagram of large needle hovering close to a tiny foetus, curled up tight as a fern, stung like a slap in the face.

I remember at some point the same nurse who had given me this information telling me, 'Really, she's just like your other two children, she'll do everything that they do, only slower,' and I puzzled at the absurdity of her statement. After their births, no one had sat down and made a prognosis of the future: broken bones, anorexia followed by addictions to illicit substances and possible heart failure in old age. And while I know that we all exist at random, that the spectre of death can single us out at any time, I had a mental script of how their lives would progress: school, college, marriage, kids—not necessarily in that order. The outline of Caoimhe's future was one I had never come across.

Over the decades scientists have gained an intimate knowledge of chromosome 21, and the 50–100 genes which live there. They know how they clog the brain's circuit board, overloading it with enzymes and proteins so that, like the mad wizard vainly manning the controls of his own effigy in the land of Oz, wires become crossed and messages confused. While I am perversely grateful that this information allows me to be alert and prepared, I am aware that the same knowledge steals something of the magic of not knowing: Caoimhe's future is not an exciting blank page; there are too many notes already scribbled in the margin.

She will not do everything my other children are able to do. She will not lose herself in the rich, infinite landscape of higher learning, nor be gripped by wanderlust and travel the world with a rucksack. She will not be a single silhouette on a Balinese beach, or trek solo through a rainforest drinking water she boiled herself on a campfire. She will not stand bemused, clutching a timetable in the middle of a dusty, chaotic Indian railway station.

I found the modern jargon used to describe Caoimhe's condition baffling. 'Retarded' was not a word in use any more; it was replaced with 'developmental delay', as if like a train running behind schedule, Caoimhe's ordinary skills would arrive eventually. While I had no doubt the basic, mechanical ones would, it was the complex, cerebral ones I grieved for. Both friends and professionals urged to me focus on the positives without dwelling on her limits, as if regret and hope, pleasure and disappointment could not coexist within my consciousness. The pendulum swung between minimising her condition and magnifying it to frightening proportions.

———

My child is not my child; she belongs to the world of science. Once she was diagnosed, she ceased to be a baby and became a medical anomaly. The curdle of my anger is ever present when I think back to how she was treated in those early months. But rage rarely bubbles up alone, and I take care not to nourish my anger, not to let it distract from the real feelings of hurt and fear and disappointment that lie beneath, open and scarlet as wounds. Diagnoses are easier, I think, if they do not come within hours of giving birth, when you are so soft and vulnerable, so easily prey to the phantom of a faraway future, frightening and alien. I wondered what societies did before the modern doctor was invented. From what I can fathom, people with extra chromosomes lived quite well within their communities. A sixteenth-century painting, Adoration of the Christ Child, in New York's Metropolitan Museum of Art, shows an angel with a flattish face and almond eyes standing next to Mary at the manger. But then came the Victorian era, and its fascination with classification, phrenology and evolution, and that eminent silver-tongued doctor John Langdon Down, who was the first to recognise certain physical characteristics and give them an identity. In 1866 he published a paper, 'The Ethnic Classification of Idiots', and it seems from that moment my daughter's fate was sealed. In my mind's eye I see Down in his white coat with a clipboard, touring the high-ceilinged corridors of the asylum in the south of England where he was the superintendent. I see him, pursed lips, brow furrowed, mind ticking, as a procession of open-mouthed idiots and grinning imbeciles is paraded for his scrutiny. I see him late at night in his office feverishly poring over mathematical indices; scribbling excitedly by candlelight before rushing home to his patient wife with the news: 'That's it, my dear! I've got it! Those smaller head circumferences . . . they're all throwbacks to an inferior sub-species of the human race!'

Down called his patients Mongolian idiots, and to vary the

theme there were Ethiopian idiots, Caucasian idiots, Aztec idiots and Malay idiots. He was their saviour, the institution their sanctuary. Down did not believe that parents were up to the task of raising their own imbeciles, arguing that 'in but few homes is it possible to have the appliances for physical and intellectual training adapted for the duration of the feeble in mind'. Down was reportedly a liberal-minded man, with a big heart and an even larger brain. He feared that the wealthier classes were embarrassed by their idiot offspring, keeping them below stairs with the servants. He could free them! At his asylum he provided refuge and restraints, opium and opulence; home was a luxurious prison, a beautiful building with its own clocktower standing in forty lush acres where inmates received the best care, bar the love and accept-ance of their families. By some divine irony Down's son Reginald, also a doctor, fathered a child with the condition, who lived happily at home until his death at the ripe old age of sixty-five. Despite this, he and his wife never really came to terms with his son's condition, not surprisingly, since Reginald, while working at the same institution as his father, concluded that the inmates might even be throw backs to the orang-utan.

I read somewhere that it was the editor of the British medical journal, *The Lancet*, who gave the condition the name 'Down syndrome' in the early 1960s. This is infinitely prefer-able to Mongolian idiot, but it's an outdated Victorian image in need of a makeover. I think the condition should be referred to by its scientific name, Trisomy 21, which sounds like a nightclub or a swish Jamie-Oliver-style eatery.

Changing the name would relieve the many health professionals who are still stumbling with Down syndrome. Plenty still make references to 'Down syndrome people', as if they must still be held hostage by their institutionalised identity.

Once, when Caoimhe was having a blood test at the Children's Hospital, the nurse, broad as a brickhouse, struggled to find a vein in Caoimhe's small, plump arm. 'Down's kids are all like this,' she muttered, her own slabs of flesh quivering with the effort. 'Bad veins.' I pointed out that I, too, have deep veins and it once took a nurse five attempts to draw blood, suggesting Caoimhe may have simply inherited my reluctant vessels. But she didn't pay any attention and continued to take aim and jab as if she was playing darts. I wrestled Caoimhe from her grip; we would try a different nurse another day. Her parting words were, 'You'd better get used to this, Down's kids have blood tests all the time.'

Whatever Caoimhe did or didn't do was as a result of Down's, it seemed. Delayed teeth, delayed walking, snoring, bizarre sleeping postures, love of music, sunny nature and big dribbly kisses came under its jurisdiction. Nothing was left for her. She was not an individual, a child as unique as her own thumbprint; she was of a different species—perhaps ape, perhaps alien—bearing identifying hallmarks which separated her from the rest of the human race and required careful handling by experts, other than her mother.

There were, of course, among the abundance of health professionals we saw, some who could see her as an individual, who would remark on a unique characteristic and in doing so allow me to savour the taste of parental pride. In these moments, when it was her hair or eyes or skin being admired, she was deliciously ordinary. But one nurse particularly annoyed me, ending each visit with a compliment about what a wonderful job I was doing. I figured this was supposed to spur me on so I would wake up the next day with renewed vigour for the Herculean task of raising a child with a disability. Instead, her vague platitudes seemed patronising, condescending, like a pat on the head.

———

I needed the raw tattered edges of emotion, not synthetic sentiment. When Caoimhe was a few weeks old, I went looking for books that could offer some guidance in unravelling the mystery of my child. I imagined the local library would have stacks of literature, but I could find only three volumes, squeezed in at the end of the burgeoning pregnancy and motherhood section, like an uncomfortable afterthought. The first was from something called the 'Special Needs Collection' and the shoutline on the front cover declared it to be 'the complete and compassionate guide written by doctors, nurses, educators, lawyers and parents'. I wonder at the pecking order. Inside, the Introduction warns: 'No book can mend a broken heart or shattered dreams,' and I see the two jagged pieces of my own heart, ruby red as a valentine's, lying among scattered bits of coloured paper. I drift through the contents and turn to 'Your Child with Down Syndrome and Your Marriage', because this is an anxiety as yet unexplored; an uneasiness, which, while not invading regular head space, sits like an anchored pirate ship, just left of the safety zone. The author, an educator, warns that children with special needs can put a strain on the relationship and a way to deal with this is to 'identify ways in which you have coped with other difficult situations in your lives. Use these same strategies in dealing with the special needs of your child with Down Syndrome.'

I think back to the time Conor and I moved to Australia, pregnant, jobless and penniless. I'd cried many tears and smashed many mugs we could ill afford to break. But comparing the two situations seemed as fruitless as the proverbial apples and pears. The truth was I'd never been in this situation before. 'Remember you, your spouse and your whole family are all in this together. Before long, your child with Down syndrome will just be part of the team.' I imagine my family as a team. I see Conor in tracksuit pants with a whistle round his neck. Me in a pinny making lemonade, the girls in short pleated skirts cheerleading a dribbling, cumbersome Caoimhe as she awkwardly lopes around a track. I shudder. I turn to chapter six, 'Your Baby's Development', and read about how important it is for me to be involved in her life, to 'maximise her potential'. I read this while my daughter lies in her cot babbling to a stuffed unicorn and I feel the twang of guilt's muscle. I go into the bedroom and make the unicorn dance and sing. She looks at me, puzzled, curious, a half-smile playing on her lips. I leave her and go back to chapter six and Developmental Milestones.

I descend the stern black bullet points with the nervousness of a student scanning an exam paper. I mentally tick off the ones she has passed, feeling relieved, then smug, until I am abruptly halted by the last one: 'Understands parent as a resource'. This is a skill she should acquire somewhere between eight and fourteen months.

By two years my child should have grasped negativism. How could she not! When Caoimhe was a few weeks old, a family friend came round with a bottle of champagne to toast her birth. With the glass in one hand, she stared down at Caoimhe and said: 'What a pity you didn't have a healthy boy.' Other friends wept when they saw her. Relatives sent cards with muted, guarded messages. They meant well, but the horror of the hospital experience had made me hyper-sensitive, as traumatised people often are. I crackled and popped like a firework, set off by the slightest comment. I revelled in being angry at other people's awkwardness, their gauche expressions of sorrow. Anger felt rejuvenating compared to the immobilising greyness of grief.

———

At odd, quiet moments I'd construct new fantasies from the shrapnel of a future bombed to smithereens: she'd be the first child with Down's to graduate from Monash University; she'd be a raging beauty, Miss Down's Universe . . . and then I'd topple them with my own hand, like a rageful toddler. Hope was built from books but smashed by reality. Chapter six went on to quote a study of children with Down syndrome who took part in an early intervention programme at an American university, and as a result, reached some develop-mental milestones 'faster than the normal child'. My goal, the book says, 'is to maximise strengths and minimise weaknesses so that your child will realise her fullest potential'. I think of my child lying supine in her cot while I sit reading about her, an armchair mother. I am failing her. I close the book.

For the rest of the day this chapter hangs like a fat little rain cloud over my future. I do not want to be involved in any sort of intervention programmes, ever. When my eldest daughter was born, I once attended a mothers' group, where we all sat cross-legged on the floor, our newborn babies placed in various containers in front, soft and pulsing like transplanted organs. One by one, we talked about how their births had changed our lives. I remember one mother sobbed uncontrollably because her child wouldn't sleep, but hers was the only expression of real emotion. As we went round the circle the same carefully constructed façade of maternal content spilled from mouth after mouth. And I confess, when it came to my turn, while I could not talk so glowingly, neither did I say: 'My life as I know it is over. I have died and am living a purgatory of bleeding nipples and haemorrhoids. My days and nights are no longer two distinct clear-cut events, but a congealed mass through which I blunder, spurred on by a cattle prod of pain.'

Like a murderer drawn to the scene of the crime, I keep returning to the book. I head to the end of the chapters where the parents have their say—after the doctors, nurses, educators, lawyers—their comments seemingly cherry-picked to add resonance to the science of the experts. Surely among my comrades I will find solidarity, empathy. But their bite-size chunks of positivity, spoken from the grimaced mouths of those with a steely ability to soldier on, only magnified my loneliness. One comment got me thinking: 'One time we were in an airport and someone came up to us and said, "Down syndrome?" When I said yes, he said, "Wonderful children, I've got one myself." It was nice of him.'

Was it? To me it served only as a reminder that my child was not just a member of my family, built from the atoms of generations of Celtic ancestors, but part of a distinctly recognisable breed, like poodles or Siamese cats. Once, when Conor was out with our three girls, he met a woman walking her dog. The woman fingered Ceridwen's curls admiringly before turning to Caoimhe and remarking brightly, 'Oh! I see she's a Down syndrome!' No one would notice her curls before her slanting eyes; she would never be seen as a regular child—she was merely an oddity, nature's mistake. The precarious wiring of her brain dictated that the order of her learning would always be awry.

I needed to know more about this changeling, to peep around the door of the future from a safe place, where I could bang it shut. Conor looted his university's library and one night we hesitantly leafed through the dubious booty. Some of the more outdated titles made us laugh: *Bernard: Raising Our Mongol Son; The World of Nigel Hunt: Diary of a Mongoloid Youth; The Psychology of Mongolism,* but there was a jagged edge to our laughter born of guilt, like laughing at bad taste jokes.

Inside the pages I'd stare at the photos of people with Down syndrome and my body would contract with fascinated horror. Here, among the anonymous black-and-white faces, I was glimpsing the caricature of Caoimhe's future and I was filled with panic: 'how can I love her if she looks like that?'.

Every waking moment I grappled with the paradox of my love for Caoimhe and my fear of her difference. It was as if her birth had stirred up schoolyard prejudices I thought I'd successfully buried; I never knew how much I needed to conform until now. I'd gone through the usual attempt at teenage rebellion, albeit a rather timid attempt: a few purple streaks, too much make-up and dressing in acres of black lace. I wanted to look alternative, but when people stared I felt self-conscious and I wished they wouldn't. I was a sparrow posing as a peacock. And now those old feelings were back. The power I had gained over my own life had been obliterated by a random act of the universe.

The uneven texture of my love only served to increase my feelings of guilt. I remember reading an article in the paper about a family raising a child with Down's. They spoke about her so lovingly, miraculously, as if she were a heavenly body. Their brave words and smiling faces chastised me from the page and I felt even more isolated.

Like the Roman god Janus, I have two faces: one etched in fear looking forward to my life ahead, the other staring mournfully at the past, eroded by the salt tears of grief for the baby I've lost. I find another book in which the author, a doctor, advises against the use of tranquillisers for mothers in shock after being given a diagnosis. I have not contemplated the use of tranquillisers, so I briefly contemplate them now. At what stage does grief become a medical condition in need of treatment? When it fogs your day, paralyses you, makes you unable to function? But how can you let it, with a new baby to look after? There is no time for grief. At night I write, to make sense of the senseless, as if transplanting the words from my head to the page will empty my mind of unwanted feelings, like putting out the rubbish. And then I read, and my brain crackles and sparks with fear. In this deceptively innocuous book there are all sorts of conditions and behaviours which the good doctor feels compelled to advise on: masturbation in public; parading one's sanitary towel in front of one's classmates; and daily care of the uncircumcised penis. I have not seen anyone, ever, masturbating in public, let alone anyone with Down syndrome. I wonder how common it is, and if it is not very common at all, as I suspect it isn't, why mention it? Because the trouble with even mentioning such things is that the idea is planted, and it grows and clings like poison ivy. As a new mother trying to make sense of my newborn baby, suddenly I am catapulted to a mortifying event fourteen years down the track: my daughter is triumphantly waving her sanitary towel for all to see, like Neville Chamberlain's doomed 'Peace in Our Time' statement.

It seems that having a medical qualification gives one the authority to hold forth on every aspect of the human condition; in this book even the basic act of washing is approached with a farcical seriousness. Under the heading 'Body Odour', the author draws attention to the important use of soap and deodorant once puberty has passed and I can only wonder what this has to do with Down syndrome. Body odour remains the scourge of society in general, so why marginalise it?

I look at the people in the photos, referred to as Miss or Mr, followed by their full name, the over-formal address a strained attempt at dignity. It seems to me that many of these medical authors may understand the scientific effects of the extra chromosome, but are no more qualified to talk on the art of parenting than the dustman. The more I read, the more I feel that all this unpleasantness and forecast of catastrophes to come have nothing to do with the baby I brought home, now lying soft and warm as a toasted muffin, full of slow, sleepy love. Still, I am uncomfortably aware that as the years go by her disability will become more conspicuous. Right at the start it took a paediatrician to confirm her difference. Now passers-by in the street stare. How long will it be before children in the playground do the same?

I continued to search for some text, some narrative, to capture my life and sing it back to me in words I understand. Someone recommends *The Down's Syndrome Handbook*, as if Caoimhe were a car, or some other piece of complex machinery which comes complete with owner manual, one I must pore over, study and digest. The book is written by a doctor whose son has the condition. This to me sounds perfect: a medical manual tempered by paternal intimacy, a personal experience weighted with knowledge. I like the tone—polite, understated, courteous. Best of all, the author raises an imaginary bushy eyebrow on the subject of intervention, warning that the studies show conflicting results with regards to any benefit. This makes me feel giddy, almost girlish, with relief, as patches of time, blue as the sky, pristine as new snow, suddenly open up before me. In this book there is no relentless positivity, no geometrically challenging exercises, just a concern with reddened purply eruptions, alopecia and patchy bald areas. But it is in the science of the chromosome that the author comes into his own, the complexity of proteins, purines, pyrimidines enthusiastically explained in layman's terms.

Still, like other scientific texts, it does not capture my thoughts and fears or give words to the stuff I am too terrified to voice. One day a friend's mother, who had worked in a special school in the north of England, sent me a yellowing copy of *Ida: Life with My Handicapped Child*, first published in Denmark in 1977. It is written by Ida's mother, who is far more concerned with prunes than purines: four a day to keep constipation at bay. In fact, her preoccupation with her daughter's bowels is a running thread throughout the book, a diverting subplot from the centre-stage drama of mental retardation: 'She starts the day seated on her potty-chair, securely harnessed, playing with her toes, blissfully ignorant of the much more serious job she is supposed to perform . . .'

What is it? The answer is revealed at 9 am when she is potted again 'with no toys except her toes. This time she seems to get the message for often within the allotted five minutes an unmistakable smell will proclaim that we have been lucky once more and saved a nappy.'

Phew. By midway through the book Ida has bowel function managed down to a fine art. But it was no mean feat in getting this far, as her mother admonishes: 'It is no doubt due to regular meals and a healthy diet with many vegetables that she is able to function this way.'

I find myself growing very attached to blond-haired Ida, plump and creamy as rice pudding. I find her metamorphosis from baby to toddler to schoolgirl-with-attitude thoroughly absorbing. By the age of six, her speech and manipulation skills are impressive: 'If you don't get me my milk right now I'll wet my pants, so there.'

In those dark days, among the dull, dry texts with their bleak prognoses, diseases and anatomical deviancies, Ida is my beacon of hope, a mascot of normality in a world of freakish possibilities. A photo of her aged thirteen shows a beautiful girl with thick, shiny blond hair and big blue eyes and I feel a surge of hope, almost painful in its intensity. Caoimhe will be beautiful too. Ida is the youngest of five children—her nearest sister is ten years older than her—but the rest of the family are no more than bit-part players in the book, as if they faded into the shadows on Ida's arrival. Teenagers, from what I hear, are as much hard work as toddlers, their demands no less exigent, their emotional lives no less tumultuous, but the dramas of Ida's siblings are rarely mentioned. Towards the end of the book is a hint, foreboding in its very lack of information, of what real life is like with a handicapped child: behind the treadwheel of diverting therapies, and the joy and relief of milestones reached is a different story of despair and anger: 'And so perhaps I ought to conclude by admitting that whatever great strides Ida has made, and however thrilled we are with her progress . . . there has been a price to pay. It has created problems for our daughter who was ten when Ida was born. She was then the youngest of four, the spoilt baby whose main function in the family up till then had been to be the little ray of sun-shine. But from then on our time and energy were taken up with Ida and the little big sister had to look elsewhere to be the centre of attention. It has therefore been, and still is, difficult for her to come to terms with the responsibility of everyday life, both in her school work and when faced with the many teenage problems and temptations of today.'

I ache to know more of this deeper, more complex story, but the subject dances lightly on the fragile surface. I discover that the girl goes to live with her aunt and cousin in a different town. 'This is also part of what Ida has cost. We can only hope that on this point the price was not too high.'

What happened dammit, what? The book ends there so I will never know. The fractured paragraphs of a troubled life create a hazy mosaic from which the true picture can only be grossly imagined. Nonetheless, there are a few pages at the back of the book where the brothers and sisters speak for themselves of life with Ida. The troubled sister talks of how as a ten-year-old she took Ida for a walk in her pram and a friend peered in and said she looked like Betty—a girl with

Down syndrome who lived in the neighbourhood and was the butt of tribal teasing. 'It was daft to say such a thing to me. I just said "Really," and walked home disappointed without telling anyone about it; instead I had a little weep in private. Nevertheless that experience was good for me.'

Brave words but a dubious truth. This is a mere taste of what I hunger for, some kernel of knowledge wrenched from its hiding place deep in the soul. In another library, I stumble across an American mother's personal account of giving birth to her daughter, Sophie, and I pounce upon it like a starved animal. I stand stock still and read, the words of pain and grief wash over me, warm and soothing as a shower, while Caoimhe, sensing freedom from my attention, demolishes the neatly-ordered bottom shelves. I take the book home; I read it at the traffic lights, in the bath, in bed, at the stove, with one hand stirring. But gradually the book becomes a source of discomfort, an accusing testament to my laziness as a parent. This woman does so much for her daughter: there are flights across the country to see specialists; vitamin formulas; brain tests and endless hours of therapy. She and her child attend classes on a daily basis and she even puts an advertisement in the paper for volunteers to come to her home every day to do some special sort of exercise, which seems to involve tying the child's limbs in elaborate knots to stimulate brain function. The pair of them also squeeze in a 'Mommy and Me' class and speech therapy once a week. All before the first birthday. I feel tired, drained and miserable. How does she do it?

There are several references to her 'wonderful husband', though I can't see what he's done that is so wonderful, other than look adoringly at the baby and shell out vast sums for therapy. I become suspicious somewhere towards the end of the book when she is pregnant with her third child and suffering dreadful morning sickness. On August 7, she conspiratorially confides: 'Sophie is napping so I've had a chance to take a shower and curl my hair. Peter is not going to recognise me. He's so used to coming home to a bedraggled tired housewife. Lately he's been crabby because the house is always messy and usually I'm lying down. On top of that I immediately hand the baby over to him as soon as he walks through the door. I can't blame the poor guy. He's been as good as is humanly possible, but even my perfect husband has his limits.' Fortunately her mother arrives just in time to rescue Peter from this suburban slum. She cleans and cooks and, thankfully, harmony is restored. Still, she tells us: 'Peter and I have a strong marriage. Each of us is the other's best friend and all in all we have the power to survive this crisis. What do other couples do?' I don't know. Curl their hair and take a shower, presumably.

I cried when I reached the end of the book. Having entered Sophie's world, even though we were in different countries and different decades, it was hard to leave, to let go. I wanted a sequel, to know what happened to Sophie, to be privy to the unwritten future. So I scoured the Internet for news of her, like some celebrity-smitten teenage fan. I found just a few references: her mum now writes restaurant reviews and Sophie is a willing accomplice with a penchant for Japanese cuisine. Her parents split up.

I am greedy for more heroines, more Idas and Sophies, to feed me with hope. I plunder the net for more memoirs and am bemused by the many references to angels—*Angel Unaware, Slant-Eyed Angel, Angel Behind the Rocking-chair, The Angel Within*—which contrast starkly with the highly medicalised 'owner manuals': *Protein Expression in the Down Syndrome Brain, Coping with Down Syndrome.* And I wonder at the stark dichotomy that exists between science and sentiment, angels and apes. I look up the word 'angel' in the dictionary: it comes from the Greek *angelos*, meaning messenger. I look at my child for signs of a hidden message from another time, another planet, another race. She stares back at me unblinkingly and then smiles. For a split second she is the teacher and I the student, gauche and overwhelmed with the task of learning, momentarily rewarded and made strong by her pleasure. I am a giant, ten foot tall, and as I grow, I see my fears shrink and lose their power. Her diagnosis transformed her into something frighteningly alien: a Victorian imbecile, a primate, a smelly being capable of outrageous behaviour—but here she is, pink and sticky with a rime of dried milk clinging to her face after yet another feed is ejected. It's mundane stuff really. My anxieties are different from the ones I cultivated in those early days, which sprang up fast as fungus and are now disintegrating spores carried off by the wind. And I feel a quiet pleasure in my victory over these marauding, shouting, internal fears.

The secret of life with Caoimhe is to hang on fiercely to the present. I have this moment, this moment right now, where I smile and she smiles and we are as separate but as tuned as notes in a scale. This is perfection. And the one thing I am certain about is that out there, in the wild, anarchic future, there will always be moments pure and fresh and unexpected as this.

In nature, change occurs slowly; she will not become an embarrassing stranger, she will never look like the photos in those outdated books. She will always be my daughter, flesh of my flesh, whom I will know intimately. And the more I realise this, the less I worry about my ability to love.

Chapter 4
Old Eggs

We sit, Conor and I, in a room at the top of a tower block. The baby lies in her pram; I am not sure if she is sleeping but she is quiet. The genetic counsellor across the table from us pushes her hair absentmindedly behind her ears, her pen sketches over the blank page in front of us. She is drawing a tree, a family tree, on which our relatives must hang, identified only by their names, ages and the afflictions and diseases that terminated their lives. My paternal grandfather, felled by senile dementia in his early seventies lies on the page next to his wife, a woman I never met and don't know much about, other than that she had heart problems and cut people's hair. Over the next few hours the branches fill, abundant as spring, as I recall the names of great-aunts and -uncles of whom I no longer have any clear mental picture, just bitty mosaics of memory: a bristly moustache, stiff as a yard brush; a large red nose with a roughened crater surface; the floured texture of doughy cheeks; shiny rock-hard nails—the body parts dance before me like dismembered puppets, fragmented caricatures of the people they once were part of, the more regular features long since forgotten. Finally the ghosts from the past are all assembled, strung out like washing, with the indelible stains of the illnesses on full display. Cancers, damaged hearts, diseases of the nervous system, afflictions that devour their identity so that their malfunctioning cells are all that is left. Occasionally there is a gap where some anonymous ancestor lies, name never known or at least only partially, but the folklore of their terrible death still livid. 'He went to the toilet and never came back!' 'He worked on the docks; fell in a vat of boiling oil!' Over the years family gatherings breathed new life onto the ashes of the faceless deceased, hot murmuring stoked the legend of their demise so that it grew and changed shape, loomed large and then shrank, but never completely disappeared from the childish mind, thrilled with the terror of death's cruelty.

———

The white sheet of paper with its lines and scribbles makes an uncomfortable picture. I am confronted by a depressing concentration of illness: my history and possibly my future. Here lies my maternal grandmother, grey-haired and plump, with a skin tag the colour of raw sausage underneath her eye. As a child I was fascinated with it; I'd run my finger over it and wobble it and wonder why it didn't come off. Fear made me remote as I watched her, some years later, succumb to Parkinson's disease, which pinned her first to her chair and then her bed, as her body rusted and buckled and finally seized up so that all that was left was a pair of moving eyeballs leaking silent tears.

Now here she is, on the page, lying next to her beloved husband, a fierce proud Welshman with a great sense of humour and an irritatingly cheerful whistle who died, suddenly, unexpectedly, while hanging his curtains.

What are we doing here, I wonder silently, desperately. I feel trapped in this sparse bright room by the sheer volume of corpses. They fill the air with their diseased presence and I struggle to breathe. It was not my idea to come. We were invited by the people who took Caoimhe's chromosomes to search for explanations to the dilemma of her existence, but the answer cannot be found in this paper graveyard, with its cancers and polyps and paralyses. There is no history of Down syndrome in either of our families and Caoimhe's trisomy is not inherited. We are plundering the past for conditions she may be vulnerable to, but the reality is she probably won't live long enough to get any of them. I am aware that her expected life span is 55 years, and that her mind may be unravelled by Alzheimer's disease long before that. Perhaps my discomfort has nothing to do with these spectres from the past; it is the future of which I am scared. I am not afraid of what old age will bestow on Caoimhe; I am sick with sadness at what it won't.

To be blunt, all I really want to know is who is responsible for her disability: my egg or Conor's sperm. The counsellor pauses. Indeed, it would be possible to examine Caoimhe's chromosomes and find out, but what would I gain from knowing, she muses carefully. I've asked myself the same question. Am I looking for the chance to point the finger? To hate Conor instead of my daughter if it were he who fired the faulty shot? To blame myself for failing my family; to hang my head in shame at my imperfectness?

Because that is how I feel. Intellectually I know this is crap, but something deep inside, something from my own past, tells me it is my fault. The ghostly wagging finger is conjured up by nearly every book I read, books which repeatedly insist that a woman's eggs are responsible in 80 per cent of cases. No wonder my shoulders slump with responsibility. I was, after all, thirty-five when Caoimhe was conceived, that magical cut-off age when one's ripe harvest begins to wither, decay. I do not feel old, but I am old. Here is the proof. My body is beginning to crack and crumble—not the visible scaffolding, but silently, creepily, on the inside, so that I am not even aware of the process. When I close my eyes and try to imagine myself internally I see blackness. I have become afraid of my own body, cut off from it. Like some Third World airline, its internal organisation is in turmoil while vainly presenting a flimsy veneer of normality.

I imagine my eggs lying in my ovaries—tough, shrivelled, frayed at the edges like dried-up offerings in a canteen. I stare at my face in the mirror and it looks back at me quizzically, a young-looking face, floating, detached from the imploding body which grew the faulty future. I examine my skin, it is still fairly elastic and smooth. I marvel at the disparity between my relatively wrinkle-free complexion and my silently perishing eggs.

I read like someone consumed, in an attempt to make sense of Caoimhe's origins. Since her birth I have gained a child's-fist grasp on the massively complicated process of reproduction, and smile at my incongruous ignorance: I know more about growing herbs than I do about this most precarious of bodily functions. It seems a million things have to go right to produce what we all take for granted.

Of course, men, too, play their part in creating children with chromosomal abnormalities, albeit a less significant one, proportional, perhaps, to their share of doing housework. The risk increases among older men, and those who do not get laid often, because sperm that is not regularly discharged eventually goes off, like old cheese. Conor is not old, nor climbing the walls of frustration, or so he assures me. Still, for a minute it is exciting to think it might not be my failing body, but his! How I wish I knew, so that my status as a healthy fertile woman can once more be unchallenged. I read until I can read no more; there are too many variables, too many theories bewildering and confusing. Down syndrome at one time or other has been linked to the pill, a lack of folic acid in pregnancy, radiation, maternal thyroid antibodies in the blood, a lack of selenium in the diet, and so on. I read until any joy I have in the baby leaks away like air from a puncture and I am left deflated. I tried so hard to have a healthy pregnancy: I ate the right foods; I guarded my health—but at the end of the day it wasn't enough. How was I to know that an Italian study showed that conceptions in spring lead to an increased risk? I chuck the paper aside in anger. Bloody academics, smug and immune in their paper towers.

This desire to know is like a guilty addiction. I scan indexes at the backs of books in shops; I trawl the net. And each day I vow to stop, to accept my lot, to love the baby I have, to give up this quest, as fruitless as the bleeding Holy Grail. But it's always a case of just one more text, one more paper, one more book will provide the answer. I think it is my own guilt that drives this relentless search. Like a frightened child, I am looking for proof that will exonerate me from the crime society has charged me with: of creating a child with a disability. I want reassurance, warm and healing as the fantasy of maternal love, that I am innocent. One day I find it. I read that in most cases of Trisomy 21, the problem with the egg occurs in the mother's own foetal life, when she herself is just

a pinprick in the uterus. I am absolved! Guilt gathers momentum as it trickles, then flows, from my veins, until I am light
and girlish once more. I did not corrupt my own eggs with
my drinking and smoking and wicked ways. It is not my fault!
It is my mother's! Again!

But this does not explain why older women are more susceptible. I read more. The egg, although formed in the foetus,
remains in a suspended stage of development until its number
is called later in life. It must reduce its chromosomal load to
make way for the sperm's passengers, but in some mothers,
it has been waiting a jolly long time for this moment and it
has started to wither, make mistakes. The cargo is already
unbalanced.

In other cases, problems occur during the act of sex when
the sperm chauffeurs in the dance partners. Conception, it
seems, is as rhythmic and orderly as a formal jig. The music
strikes. The dance begins. The partners approach each other
across the crowded cell of the egg and once aligned, are supposed to stick to each other with the aid of something called
chiasma, non-genetic strands, which are sticky, like flypaper.
It is this stuff, apparently, that becomes inefficient with age
and loses its goo, so that the chromosomes fail to adhere.

And it's here the capers end. The body shudders at such
asymmetric disharmony and calls a halt. The performers are
brutally dismissed—they are flushed down the vagina—and
next month the dance may begin again. This is the reality for
80 per cent of babies with Down's—life is over before it has
barely begun.

One book clinically refers to this as the process of selective
destruction, and snootily remarks on some women's inability
to recognise their own mistakes and correct them. I feel

chastised. Foolish body! Clinging to its faulty cargo, singing lullabies to reject stock. Love is truly blind.

Still, I can't help wonder why I held on to Caoimhe. Did my body know, at some subliminal level, of her difference? Surely not, otherwise it would have expelled her, wouldn't it? For to hold on to her while 'knowing' would go against the law of evolution, the survival of the fittest, an ancient tenet embedded in the earth's crust on which the sentimental modern myth of maternal instinct grows rampant like some feral weed.

Perhaps it was because we planned her being so carefully that my stubborn body refused to let go. To do so would have shattered my carefully constructed façade of control. God, we took such a business-like approach to her conception: dates, times, money and futures, and plans, damned plans, hatched over candlelight. So earnest we were, I laugh at myself now. In the quiet of the evening, we discussed who'd work and who'd stay home; whether we'd need a bigger car; how we'd survive financially—but we never discussed the possibility of disability.

Even so, we were not entirely naive. Many years ago I had a laparoscopy which revealed widespread pelvic scarring. Unbeknown to me, blood had been collecting and congealing in my uterine cavity, sticking to my organs, ploughing my pelvis with long ridges of scar tissue, hinging it backwards. My fallopian tubes were a labyrinth of wrong turns and culs-de-sac; a healthy conception, the surgeon warned me, would require medical assistance. Indeed, any conception ran a very strong risk of developing in the tubes, ending the baby's life and putting mine at risk. This information was delivered briskly by a man in a white coat in a cold room at a Dublin maternity hospital. 'But don't rely on it for contraception,' was his parting shot, delivered with a smile thin and stiff as a dried twig. As I left through the main doorway, still reeling, a heavily pregnant mother arrived groaning with the intensity of labour. I felt a stab of pain that was an amalgam of grief, longing and jealousy for something I had always blithely assumed would be mine when I wanted it, but had now been taken away. I had not longed for children, I had hardly given them a second thought, but now they filled my head: small girls with flying pigtails, solemn boys in woolly hats—my offspring who must remain trapped in my fantasies. 'We can always adopt,' said Conor as he drove through the wet streets in his battered silver Toyota. 'Yeah,' I said, but at that moment I did not want to adopt. I wanted to be pregnant, to feel my own baby growing inside my imperfect, ravaged body.

It was three months after this hospital bombshell that I went to India to interview Mother Teresa for a Sunday paper. It was my greatest journalistic coup, one I had spent months organising, making frustrating phone calls to Calcutta on crackling lines which kept cutting out. Once I was there, it was something of an anticlimax; I felt overwhelmingly tired and dizzy as I trudged the wet, sweaty streets, unable to enjoy the buzz which usually accompanies a challenging interview. 'Why are you not married?' Mother Teresa asked me at the end of our meeting. 'No one will have me,' I joked lamely, thrown by the unexpectedness of the question. 'Come back and work for me as a Little Sister of the Poor,' she chuckled, and I smiled. With the very real possibility of a barren and childless future ahead, I felt as empty as a nun.

Loss was weighing heavy on me that week, perhaps because I was staying at a home for rescued street children. I would sit on the floor of the crumbling building and watch them running, shouting, laughing, crying—emotion colouring the humid air. There was one fourteen-year-old who sat quietly, saying nothing. She had burned away her throat swallowing bleach. Too physically traumatised to speak, she communicated with her eyes, which were unusually expressive. I was stirred by conflicting thoughts: sadness at what had been done to these children; pleasure and awe in the triumph of their survival; anger at what desperate parents are capable of; and fear too, at the responsibility of shaping the foundations of a life.

In the airport on the way home I drank a bottle of Kingfisher beer. It tasted metallic. Back in Dublin I became very sick. I was hospitalised in case I had picked up some strange virus from the streaming gutters, but tests, including chest x-rays, did not throw up anything insidious. Neither did they reveal my tiny unexpected daughter, who had somehow manoeuvred herself through the twisted channels of my blocked tubes and washed up on the shores of the uterus, her nascent self a triumph of survival. Three and a half years later my second daughter, like a bagatelle ball, also cannoned her way to safety.

When I became pregnant a third time, I dutifully went for a blood test to check the hormone levels which would indicate that the baby was developing normally. I was half-afraid we couldn't be so fortunate again. The blood test revealed what I feared: there was something wrong. I imagined the baby ensnared in the scar tissue her sisters had managed to avoid, being tossed about, like flotsam, before being caught on a crevice. Perhaps she had found shelter in one of the many potholes and would cling to the spot and grow; perhaps this was the ectopic pregnancy I so feared.

In those first few weeks, when my blood was scrutinised every other day, I hardly dared move. I went to the doctor's surgery and then home. My face was a mask, bearing expressions as strange and as exaggerated as a puppet's. I would catch sight of it in the mirror while I was playing with my children and see that it registered simple fake emotions that did not correlate with the squall that raged beneath. In my head I was fixated with my secret internal life; I would stare at my midriff and mentally track the baby's progress. Where are you? I'd ask. Here? Here? When the doctor warned that miscarriage was imminent, I wrote the baby a letter to say goodbye, but deep down I was willing her to live. Hang on, hang on, I pleaded. I had an ultrasound, and suddenly she was transposed to the monitor above me: oddly detached, a grey dot who had landed triumphantly in the uterus.

She had made it, but, as I have already mentioned, with blood seeping around the cavity, no one thought she would be there long. When the second scan a week later picked up the weak beat of her heart, I imagined her exhausted with the struggle of survival but I still couldn't let her go. Hang on, hang on. I wonder now, how much influence did I have on her life? If I hadn't willed her to live would she have slipped away gratefully? I could have tried again in a few more months, with a different egg. But I wanted this baby. This egg.

At eight weeks when we found out that Caoimhe was as healthy as an embryo could be, with a strong heartbeat and a good chance of survival, the doctor who performed the scan said congratulations. It was the first time anyone had had the confidence to say so. But the scars of those early weeks stayed with me; whenever I thought of the baby's future it was clouded with shadow. I tried to make sense of it, but not too

much. I don't know if I wanted to know. I remember at some
point in the pregnancy seeing a photograph of a man and
woman and an almond-eyed toddler with burnt gold hair in
bunches. They were a laughing troika; the child was between
them swinging on their hands. I felt a fierce surge of love. After
Caoimhe was born I looked for the picture but I couldn't find
it among the abundance of baby manuals which warp our
bookshelf with their weight. Recently when I looked at
Caoimhe, with her gold brown hair in pigtails, I wondered if
I had somehow foreseen her.

But I am running ahead. Back in the tower block, in that
stiflingly bright room, the baby is still lying quietly, pale as
spilt milk, oblivious to the concerns of her existence that
plague her mother's waking hours. The counsellor has finished sketching. I have no more questions. I am outwardly
calm and civilised, but something inside wants to tear the
page from the desk, to rip it up and crush the shards, because
my daughter is just a few months old yet she has already met
with death and chosen life. I am not ready to gird myself once
more against her loss.

——

Two hours have passed. The counsellor tells us we will never
know what happened, what processes went awry when she
was summoned into being. We go home. Over the next few
weeks I find myself looking at Caoimhe, puzzling, fathoming. I
know more about her genetic make-up than I do the others,
I know her chromosome pattern, the date she was conceived,
the very hour, in fact. I am familiar with the crazy paving

smudge of her thumbprint and the diseases to which her
altered body is susceptible. I have seen her grow from a winking dot on a computer monitor, I know her every measure-
ment—but there is a part of her that remains mysterious,
unreachable, unexplainable. Here is this new life carved from
me; like a Russian babushka doll I'd opened up expecting to
find a baby that was, in part, an extension of me, my
immortality. Instead there is an alien in the crib, a changeling,
even the skin cells of this creature are different. She cries and
her marbled arms reach up to me. I smile and scoop her up,
my lips brush the side of her head, I sing and she is soothed.
It doesn't matter what nonsense I put to music, the wave of
my voice is narcotic. But there is a sadness in our embrace
that I feel for us both; whatever I give her will not be passed
on; she will not have children of her own. The slow and
timely procession of myself through generations has come to
an abrupt halt with Caoimhe. Children carry forward what
they learn from the past: they grow, leave, and make their
own families, but Caoimhe's face will always be turned to
mine. I wonder how she will feel about not being a mother,
not experiencing this, what she has given me. It seems too
cruel that I can revel in this bottomless depth that envelopes
me when I hold her, this maternal bliss that she will never
have. Puppies, kittens, nieces, nephews can be held and loved
and cared for but it will never feel like this.

It dawns on me that this need to understand the origins of
her existence is about making her normal; I am disappointed
that science cannot remove the mystery, cannot stop my
imagination running away from me. Sometimes I wonder,
bizarrely, if she is not the creation of an earthly union,
mine and Conor's, but the result of some supernatural

implantation, like Jesus, or the alien, V. But I remember the
sex we had to create her, so perfectly planned we forgot
the passion, and this is the result. With our other two, I don't
remember having a single adult discussion about the effect of
babies on our lives, but the memory of their conceptions can
still produce a secret smile, a wicked inner warmth: there was
salt in the air, red wine and magic, an electricity which fused
them into being.

That was all missing for Caoimhe. When I look at her I see
every row, every spitted heated word, every flaw in our
relationship encompassed in her mal-assembled body; like a
biblical scapegoat her mottled skin is the woven cloth of our
failings, her erroneous features the scars of our fights.

Conor will protest when he reads this. No! It is not like
that! She is just a little girl with a disability, as much our
daughter as the others. He sees truth where I project fear. But
he has not grown her inside, felt the first stirrings, delicate as
the beat of butterfly wings, giving way to stronger, sturdier
limbs drumming impatiently against the prison flesh. He has
not indulged in secret conversations with a child who turned
out to be a mere illusion, just a fantasy of the mind, who
vanished the moment this changeling came, as callously as a
cold-hearted lover. Like Alice in Wonderland, I was conned;
I believed I was carrying a baby but on closer inspection it
was a pig that lay squawking in the Duchess's arms.

Caoimhe is my stigma, one I must bear alone. She is the
outward sign of internal biological turmoil, a mistake, a
product of a union that is less than perfect. She is the placard
that declares our family defective. Once when we strolled out
with our two beautiful girls, we were greeted with admiring
smiles and comments; like some impressionist work of art we

were gazed upon favourably. Now the painting is irrevocably altered; there is an ugly stain on the canvas, a rip in the tableau, as if someone has come along and splattered it with ink, or taken a knife to it, and in doing so, revealed what we had managed to conceal for so long: that we are not picture-perfect. Hate, anger, frustration, disappointment curdle under the façade of happiness, feelings and emotions which inhabit the darkest corners of everyone's home but are rarely allowed to be seen.

Now when I venture out, my chin juts just a little bit more, my demeanour is slightly defensive as I guard myself instinctively against those whose mistakes are not so visible: the picture-perfect families we once were too. It is so much harder in this consumer-crazed bubble of wealth where I live, this bayside suburb of Melbourne where blond-haired, A-grade children are the ultimate commodity; where twins come late in life from a test tube, selected, screened and sterilised like jars of bland baby food; where the unspoken belief is that children like Caoimhe, at the very least, should be confined to housing association flats in poorer areas, where money cannot barter with nature, and cash transactions cannot stamp out life's difficulties.

———

How bitter I sound. As if IVF babies have not sprung from the heartache of infertility, or are without their own vulner-abilities. But, as I have already said, it is easy to get marooned on misery island. Anyway, there is something else happening, something good. I am becoming more conscious of my own appearance.

My clothes are becoming brighter; there are colours and ribbons and tribal painted skirts instead of worthy polar fleeces and sombre tones that hide stains. I bin the bottle-green cardigan. I hate it. I raid the junk shops for lime green trousers, purple striped flares, glittery orange tops. The colours clash. My hair grows long and I wear it in plaits from which bits keep escaping. My eldest daughter is alarmed by the change and aches for the familiar mum in the sensible jeans with the controllable haircut. But I am straining at the binds of motherhood, impatient to discover what for so long has been lost: colour, youth, gaiety.

In another of life's contradictions, having Caoimhe has unearthed something that got buried after the first birth: a sensuality that went underground as I dutifully donned the dreary garb of motherhood, with just a small sigh, following in the footsteps of generations of women as if there was really no choice. One day I take Caoimhe to a new playgroup in the wealthy suburb where I live. As we sit in a ring apart from our children I feel panic palpable in my chest. I am surrounded by 'mothers', women who long ago surrendered their sensuality in favour of a bland persona, which offers muffins and freshly ironed shirts, but not much else. The talk is about the play-group vacuum cleaner. It has broken down again, because some people just don't know how to treat it. I realise that for a long time I have not known how to treat myself. I look at Caoimhe; she is the other side of the room playing with a mess of musical instruments. She is a sticky contrast to the neat white heads of the other children: there is a sock missing and snot, thick as treacle, oozing from both nostrils. Her pigtails are stiff with porridge. She catches me smiling at her and grins back, her face alive with the raw unburnished act of living. The look she gives me is so vibrant, so naked, so strong, I shrink from it. I am weak with the responsibility of defending this moment, of fighting off experiences that may dull the radiance, tarnish it. I am aware that the best way to protect her is to protect myself, to fight for the prize of an adult sexuality and hang on to it, grimly, determinedly, in a society all too keen to diminish it.

I've read about yummy mummies, with their Botoxed foreheads and their Jimmy Choos and I don't want to be one. But neither do I want to be the mother of a child with Down syndrome. Old. I remember a friend remarking to me that I didn't look like a mother of a child with Down's and I had to stop and think about it. What was such a woman supposed to look like, I asked. 'Grey,' she said. 'Sensible. Elasticated.' I unearth a book, a photographic essay of reproduction, and note that my edition was published in 1993. There, at the back, tucked away behind the sun-tanned youthful couples cavorting on beaches, is a section on chromosome abnormalities, illustrated with a photo of a mother hugging her naked toddler; the mother's beige hair was rigorously coiffed; she wore a pair of yellow slacks and a wistful expression on her ageing, downturned face. The message was clear: she was old, she was sad and about as sexual as a leaking bucket.

Perhaps, then, this re-emergence of a younger, more colourful imprint of myself is nothing more than a defiant attempt to buck the trend, a pathetic fuck-you gesture to the world, a sign that I wasn't going to go down, become a member of the coiffed-helmet brigade. Perhaps it was merely a bid to separate myself from my flawed child, to put some distance between us so that the label of her disability does not attach itself to me. Who knows. I was brought up to believe that sexuality was to be feared, and in mothers abhorred. As a teenager I railed against the constraints of my convent school. I spent many an hour arguing heatedly over the religious nonsense of a sexless Madonna, but how slowly and blindly I have succumbed to her magnetic force. I am up to my neck in the mire of motherhood and only now am I aware of the disparity between what the mouth has been saying and the way I've been living. Like some religious nut with a sandwich board proclaiming 'Jesus Saves', while the ship goes down, I have been spouting feminist mantras while emotionally succumbing to the inevitable plight of my own mother and hers before that. My appearance, my career, my preoccupations with cleanliness, sterilising, cooking, the state of the toilet, the need to have everything perfect, I see now mask an anxiety about how to be a mother and remain sexual. Jesus, I am seconds away from caring about vacuum cleaners.

But look! I am fighting back, clawing free from her grasp and those of the dead female ancestors on the tree who still exert such a force on my life. I am alarmed at how far I have sunk, how close I am to being totally submerged in a culture I blithely vowed would not change me. How did this happen? How can the intellect remain firm in one set of beliefs and the subconscious fixed in another? I see a yawning gap between my emotional and intellectual life, a chasm I must work to close, and the task is daunting.

I never went back to that playgroup, unable to face the expensive tracksuits, the hollowness of shiny nails and dyed blond hair. I do not fully understand how Caoimhe's birth has reawakened this dormant sexuality, but I am grateful to my daughter. She may be the symbol of a flawed union, of an ageing body, but she has delivered a message from my soul, has freed me from my past. She is not part of a picture-book society, full of toddlers with neat, white-blond hair and bright, jelly-sweet clothes, perfectly ironed, but my love for her at this moment is unswerving, undiminished. She is beautiful in her imperfectness. We both are. It has taken me a while to learn to love my body again after the crush of failure, but I do with a new tenderness. I am kinder on myself. This is what having Caoimhe has taught me. Learning to love her has taught me how to love myself.

Chapter 5
Beauty and Grace

At the age of eleven, I was plucked from the grass-and-gravel world of my junior school and sent to an all-girls establishment run by the nuns. Up until that point in my life, I'd no real experience of Catholicism, other than a lingering disapproval passed down by my Protestant parents, who objected to the grandeur and ostentation of the churches and to the amount of importance given to Mary, who was 'only the mother, after all'.

I am not sure, then, why they sent me to a school so at odds with their sparse Methodist beliefs. Anyway, I suddenly found myself in a world of echoing corridors where dark shapes flitted silently as bats and the chipped plaster faces of statues stared down from their lonely pedestals, beseeching, reproaching.

For me, Catholicism was an eerie, uncomfortable world dedicated to hours of prayer: meaningless monotone chants strung out by plastic beads and occasionally broken up by the baffling eloquence of Latin verse. My abiding memory of school life is those endless prayers, offered up to a heaven crowded with saints: blank and mysterious as dolls to a child. St Joseph for help with exams; St Medard for dry weather on excursion day; and my old friend St Jude, the patron saint of Hopeless Cases and Things Despaired Of. I was sceptical that these prayers would do any good. Experience had taught me that grown-ups were not very good at listening to children; I doubted that dead ones could do a better job. But the school commanded conformity, so every day I dutifully performed these dull monologues like piecework; I may as well have been on an assembly line, such was my emotional response. Even the nuns, I suspect, got little out of prayer any more: the older ones would shuffle their feet and look at their watches, thirty-odd years of repetition having worn them down like limestone.

The most tedious prayer was the Angelus, performed on the dot of midday, when in unison we would rise to our feet, turn and face the eastern wall of the classroom and begin in a dull resigned harmony: 'The Angel of the Lord declared unto Mary and she conceived of the Holy Spirit . . . blah blah blah.' After the first line I was gone, in a trance, the words a cue to vacate the learning part of my brain and journey to a different landscape. Unfortunately the eastern wall was not a blank canvas on which to project my daydreams; the middle was interrupted by a copy of the Renoir painting, *The Umbrellas*, and my eyes were often drawn to it, thoughts and ideas lost to its commanding presence. Over the years I became well acquainted with the small girl in the painting, the one with the dark eyes, who waited for me every day, who would stare back, mocking me in my daily drudgery. Not for her a world of stale words and meaningless repetition; she was young enough to be free. Still in charge of her own life, which ran like clockwork under her infantile rule, she radiated an imperialist confidence born of the knowledge that she was utterly adored. Standing above, her mother's face displays amused indulgence as she looks down on the child; another figure, perhaps her sister, stands just to the left: her

Caoimhe at 14 weeks old: 'Her smile starts at the top and spreads downwards so her whole face beams.' John Donegan/Fairfax Photos.

Caoimhe, aged 14 months, joining in at Wynnie's Kindergarten, Carnegie, Melbourne. With thanks to Lisa Minogue.

This shot was taken at Lake Mountain, Victoria, about two hours north-east of Melbourne. Caoimhe is one year old and enjoying her first taste of snow.

Autumn festival at Wynnie's Kindergarten. Caoimhe enjoys the rustle of gold.

Ellie, Wynnie and Caoimhe in our garden in Brighton, Melbourne. Caoimhe is triumphantly waving a broken ceramic angel which she has just dug up from the rose bush.

Me and Caoimhe at home in Piggery Heights.

01/04/2006

Caoimhe and her friend Luke spinning webs in Cindy's kitchen, Co. Down.

Caoimhe discovers her jump in the farmyard at Piggery Heights.

Wearing her new glasses in Nana's garden, Dundalk, Co. Louth.

Caoimhe and her two sisters, Ellie and Wynnie.

Braving the winter cold in the lakeside gardens at Mount Stewart, Co. Down.

Feeding the ducks with Papa at Stephenstown Pond, near Dundalk, Co. Louth.

Caoimhe and Lucy chilling out in the hammock in our garden in Australia. Caoimhe is five and happily readjusting to the Australian way of life. The dogs have got the hang of things too.

face is obscured, but you can tell from the tender way she
rests her left arm on the child's shoulder that she, too, is
ensnared in the conspiracy of omnipotent love.

'Hail Mary, Full of Grace, the Lord is with Thee. Blessed art
Thou among Women and Blessed is the fruit of Thy womb,
Jesus.' Oh, how many more. A stifled yawn. The wizened nun is
staring at the floor, her lips reduced to a rubbery mumble; the
beginning and end of the words melt away and the ooze that
flows from the slit of her mouth is shapeless and unbroken
like slurry. My stomach rumbles. The girl in the painting
stares smugly, her pink and white cheeks soft as a piglet's.
Lunch for her is only a tantrum away. 'Pray for us now, and at
the hour of our death. Amen.'

Release. Relief. Lunch. A sausage sandwich or a pork pie, or
whatever carrier of saturated fat my mother could get her
hands on that morning. Still, the ordeal of having to pray for
it, to stand, with rumbling stomach for what seemed like eons,
means it is always gratefully received, even when I am the butt
of jokes from my well-heeled classmates whose lunchboxes
do not betray working-class roots, as does mine. Real ham,
they have, nothing potted or from a tin. And dried fruit! And
then in the chaos of the canteen—the sniping, the laughter,
the comfort of familiarity—the bell rings and we are
summoned back to those eerily quiet corridors where the
silence is occasionally punctured by the muffled shouting of
an exasperated teacher as some poor dolt chokes on the de-
hydrated knowledge we are force-fed, like geese being fattened
for foie gras. After a mind-numbing afternoon, we stand and
pay homage once more to Mary before our release at ten
minutes to four, precisely. No wonder she is full of grace; like
a petrol tank she is never allowed to go empty. Our tedious

round-the-clock supplications keep her running smoothly.

I wonder what it's like to be full of grace. What exactly is grace, other than a brown word with shades of grey? It's a diverse word, an umbrella term: according to the dictionary it has fifteen different meanings. Was Mary full of 'elegance and beauty'? 'Charm'? 'Goodwill and favour'? Did she offer a 'sense of propriety and consideration for others', or was it 'mercy and clemency' the angel had in mind when he uttered those immortal words?

After leaving school, I never gave grace much further thought, until we were choosing Caoimhe's name. Hers is an ancient Celtic one, probably originating from County Armagh in the north of Ireland, and it means beauty and grace. There's even a seventh-century saint with her name, though I am not sure what patronage she bestows on us poor flawed mortals. She is a lesser-known saint, not on the same celestial sphere as her revered counterparts, say, Teresa or Bernadette.

It was Conor who chose her name, during the winter of pregnancy, when I was too preoccupied with keeping breakfast down to care too much about what to call the source of my sickness. In the evenings, Conor would offer up little lists like the Queen to Rumplestiltskin: if she had been a boy, she may have been a Seamus, Fionn or Gryffydd; when we discovered she was a girl, Maeve, Tara, Niamh, Carys and Bethan were briefly considered, but her diaspora of cousins had already laid claim to most of them. From around the sixth month, Caoimhe surfaced and eventually stuck. After we discovered she had Down syndrome, I wondered, briefly, wildly, how she would ever spell it; no one in the hospital seemed to be able to manage it, and the paediatrician who gave us the diagnosis even gave up trying to pronounce it, and referred to her simply as 'Baby'. But Conor was adamant that the name, and its bewildering jiggle of vowels, stay with her. The rest of the world may struggle with the spelling, but not her. She would triumph over the faltering pens of bureaucrats, the tripping tongues of medics. She would teach them something they did not know. I wasn't so sure; I have had a lifetime of spelling out my name, Kathryn—no, with a K, and an r–y–n at the end—and I find it an exasperating process. (I looked up a 'saints' site on the web and found St Drogo, patron saint of speech difficulties, who she can pray to for help in conquering this tough verbal hurdle.)

When Caoimhe was aged 19 months, before she had even attempted to say her name, she began to walk; she took her first steps in the playroom when her entourage was present: sisters, mother, father.

Unlike other babies, she more or less bypassed the 'cruising' phase in which they walk around the edges of a room grimly clinging to bits of furniture like miniature abseilers. Instead, she crawled into the middle of the playroom, her domain, slowly positioned herself vertically, and then took six steps, like a zombie, arms outstretched, legs stiff with effort. Her body was unwieldy and awkward as a plastic doll's as she determinedly made her way across the room towards me. But oh, her face! The look of pristine joy in this most mundane of achievements; the surprise which fractured her features with pleasure; the pink wet tongue that protruded with effort; the eyes which were further slanted with crinkly delight. And watching her, a warmth descended over me, sudden as a visitation, and I glowed in it, basked in it, as if a door had been opened and I could see the kernel of the world, the powerhouse where emotions and feelings are generated and dispersed. For a moment I felt a love of boundless magnitude, a sense of wellbeing, a knowledge of my place in the world, a connectedness with all beings. I resonated with the cosmos. It was as if my own shining soul had revealed itself to me, as if life's rubble had toppled aside and there it was, glinting underneath like buried treasure. Unfortunately, this experience only lasted a few minutes, and then I was back to being the unravelled, bewildered, flawed creature I am so familiar with, but in that timeless space, that interface between episodes of reality, I understood what it was to be Mary, to be full of grace.

In the course of Caoimhe's short life there have been many more moments like these. I imagine most people who have raised a child will be familiar with them. What makes mine so intense is the sheer unexpectedness of them. Nobody talks about the exquisite feelings that can be part of raising a child with a disability, and my rapturous pleasure felt forbidden, almost shameful. People feel sorry for parents of disabled children, and I have learnt to expect pity. This all-consuming joy feels like a secret, one I cannot talk about, because people may think I am odd. I would not have expected to experience anything like this from a child I considered so profoundly different. I imagined that parents of children with disabilities carried a daily burden of martyrdom and duty, which in turn would offer a sort of masochistic pleasure, a muted happiness obtained by default—but not this naked bliss.

———

Perhaps it is the backdrop of suffering that gives these moments their brilliance. Perhaps it helps that Caoimhe is so beautiful. I heard of a study in which researchers set about proving the Darwinian notion that good-looking children were more loved than their homely siblings. Mothers at supermarkets were secretly watched and it was discovered that plain children were allowed to stray farther from their parents than pretty ones.

To me this sounds flawed. Doesn't every mother think her child is a work of art? I am always agog at the mothers in shopping centres who queue in quivering excitement to enter their child in a Bonny Baby competition, when it is obvious that their offspring bears a close resemblance to a gargoyle. Perhaps, like the fairy queen in *A Midsummer Night's Dream*, when our children are born we are sprinkled with a magic potion which makes us love them, no matter what. Like Titania, maybe I was enamoured of an ass, but there were times when I did think Caoimhe was truly beautiful. I spent many minutes staring in awe at her perfect skin and the limpid eyes that linked her to another world. I felt her beauty like a pain: was I, too, once this flawless? I ached with the responsibility of protecting such purity, unworthy of such a gargantuan task. When she cried, I held her and she was immediately soothed; she was a lot more confident of my capabilities than I was. When she was asleep, I could look at her freely once there was distance between us and marvel at what Conor and I, neither of us great oil paintings, could produce. My other two daughters drew admiring comments wherever we went: Wynnie's curly hair like a headful of happy springs; Ellie's luminous grey-green eyes, changeful as a forest floor, and I lapped it up. Because much as we like to deny it, our children are our achievements. When people complimented the girls, I glowed with pleasure and silently deposited the remarks in my bank of self-esteem. I was rich. There's an entire culture out there that supports the opinion that children are what mothers make them, from Freud to Fred Bare. If I take credit for their good looks and model behaviour, who will shoulder the blame when things go wrong?

Me, of course. When Caoimhe was given her diagnosis it was as if she had been doused in tar, her beauty cruelly, dramatically obscured. As I've already noted, Down syndrome strikes at the heart of two of society's most important foundations: intelligence and looks. Over the years, social conditioning has instilled in me that people with Down syndrome are not good-looking; at best, they are plain. Thick necks; protruding tongues; mottled skin, dry as a lizard's; thin sparse hair cut in a functional pudding bowl style. And they are fat, of course.

Now, when I looked down at Caoimhe I could only see defects where minutes ago there was perfection. Her beautiful almond eyes belonged to an alien, her ears were deformed, her neck thick and wrinkled. She was not beautiful at all. She was ugly. Open any book on Down syndrome and it will clinically describe the 120 or so characteristics to which Caoimhe is vulnerable: 'malformed ears', 'flat face', 'odd-shaped teeth'. I am not alone in the conclusion that my child is a scar on the landscape.

Perhaps this is why children with disability are rarely seen in the media. As a society we do everything we can to preserve our fantasies of beauty. Only children who look as if they have been made from a hundred and one flavours of ice cream are allowed to be on show. They are not just selling the product; they are selling a dream—the dream of the perfect family.

For the purpose of this chapter, I decide to gather evidence: I scour a magazine, looking for advertisements for child model agencies, and ring one to see what their reaction would be to representing a child with Down syndrome. I dial the number nervously and swallow my morals; this is research.

A cheery female voice answers. 'Do you take children with Down syndrome?' My words trip over themselves in a garbled rush of embarrassment. 'Yes,' says the woman, sounding a little taken aback. 'Are you thinking from a weight perspective?'

Indignation flares, like a prodded dog. How could she assume my child was fat? 'No,' I say, shortly, tersely. She pauses. 'How old is the child?' she asks, her voice kindly, reassuring. 'Twenty-two months,' say I, slightly mollified by her tone. Now it is her turn to seem surprised. 'Is that all? Can I ask why you are ringing?' And then I look down at the advertisement and I am suffused with scarlet. I have dialled a weight-loss programme. I apologise, hang up and try again.

The woman who answers this time pauses for a split second before smoothly moving into second gear. She goes off to talk to the manager. She comes back with the message: 'Don't waste your money.' They don't have any children with disabilities on their books and have never been asked for them by their clients. 'It might be nice to have one,' she says, but the joining fee is over $200 and is there any point if she won't get work?

'How old is your little girl?' she asks.

'Twenty-two months.'

'Sweeeeeeet!'

This cloying assessment of a child she has never met, vowels elongated like the whine of a mosquito, is my consolation prize and cue to exit. I hang up, awash with relief that the ordeal is over. Child models and their mothers make me shiver at the best of times. Later I can chew and spit out the contents of our conversation, prod and dissect the sentences, make sense of what she was trying to say, which ultimately amounted to rejection at the first post.

Of course, this isn't proper research. Maybe if I phoned a dozen model agencies there might be one or two prepared to take Caoimhe on. But somehow I doubt it. The plain truth is that she is at odds with society's concept of beauty. She will never be anyone's fantasy child and as a grown-up she is unlikely to conform to society's strict requirements. She is a stain on the beauty world's landscape; she contradicts that to which we all must aspire. She represents our own insecurities: no jawline, round shoulders, stubby limbs. She doesn't fit and she never will. In a world where women starve themselves, risk their lives under surgery to mould themselves into an unrealistic image, it's no wonder people like her are despised and segregated. She represents all the flaws we fear and loathe in our own bodies.

I once spent a few weeks shadowing a plastic surgeon for a feature I was writing for a newspaper. My first job was to watch him shrink someone's large and pendulous breasts, the cause of much grief. At the start of the operation, as the woman lay naked and lifeless in the operating theatre, two nurses, heavily made-up and with gold earrings glinting under the operating lights, appraised her ample bosom. 'Two sacks with a golf ball at the bottom,' said one. 'Saggy, very saggy,' agreed the other. 'She says they keep her armpits warm at night.'

Forty minutes later the right breast, which had nursed two children, lay deflated and in bits, the nipple marooned in a sea of raw skin. 'Sometimes we wonder how we are ever going to get them back together, but we always do,' one of the nurses confided. I watched as the nipple was realigned, stapled to the breast, trimmed and stitched into place. Instead of flopping to the side, it pointed to heaven. 'Now that,' said the surgeon, staring approvingly at his handiwork, 'is a nice breast.'

———

Afterwards, in his opulent padded office, furnished with the woes of imperfection, we talked about his work, which was, he said, all about 'normalising' people's appearance, so they fitted better into society, felt more comfortable and had greater self-esteem. What is a normal appearance?, I asked. He shrugged. His website, however, suggested that a good candidate for breast enlargement was a woman whose 'clothes fit well around the hips but are often too large at the bustline'. Similarly, you could be considered for a forehead lift if you had 'low position of the eyebrows, creating a tired, sad appearance'.

A week later, I watched a 35-year-old woman, suffering from the tired, sad look, undergo keyhole surgery to lift her brow. Three incisions were made across the top of her head and a long thick metal rod inserted to detach the flesh from the bone. It wasn't a delicate procedure; there was an ominous scraping sound as the rod hit the bone. And then came the gory bit. A couple of small biodegradable screws were drilled into her head—specially designed so they wouldn't enter the brain—and the detached brow was hitched 5 millimetres higher. Scarlet tributaries of blood began sliding down her long black hair, splashing onto the tiles beneath. There was something of the amateur horror movie about the scene: she lay there with her manicured nails polished candy pink and the top of her head prised open. I felt anxious.

Why on earth do women do this to themselves? The risks are substantial. Pain, infection, scarring, nerve injury and even death. I had been asked to write this story after the novelist Olivia Goldsmith, author of the *The First Wives Club*, died undergoing a chin tuck. The medicalisation of the beauty industry is now big business. But most of us in some way fall short of society's unattainable gold standard. I wonder uneasily if we are not just pathologising normality by suggesting our shortfalls are problems to be fixed.

The problem I see with cosmetic surgery is that the end products are so homogeneous. The image being peddled has become the mould from which we should all be manufactured. When it gets too wrinkled, the face, the blueprint of our identity, is rubbed out and refashioned. No longer a map of our life, it becomes a road to nowhere. Despite the roar of feminism, studies show that the better-looking candidate, rather than the better-qualified one, gets the job. Dating remains a survival of the prettiest. In Australia there are now more tertiary-educated single women than equivalently educated men. If you want to get noticed, best cut off your nose if it spites your face.

Long after I wrote the article, anxiety continued to gnaw. I felt anger towards the Botox babes, the women who sit in nail bars, paying someone lots of money to massage their cuticles. Where does my girl fit in a culture whose currency is looks? How will she survive in a place where people are willing to risk death to fall within the parameters of a pseudo normality? Because nobody looks like the images thrust on us by the media which digitally sculpts fantasies and projects them as real. As the 'supermodel' Cindy Crawford once said, 'I wish I looked like Cindy Crawford.' I fear most for

Caoimhe's teenage years, when she will look at her slim, pretty contemporaries and feel envy and pain; when she will dance in front of the mirror trying to emulate some polished plastic popstar, some crude imitation of beauty, and cry because she can't. I fear that she will be intelligent enough to know she doesn't fit, but not cognitive enough to understand why. She will exist only in the margins of society, her disability will keep her confined to the shadows, where she won't have to be seen.

I read somewhere that the Egyptian philosopher Plotinus believed that an obsession with physical beauty is a sign of arrested development. The true value of physical beauty, he considered, was that it alluded to something beyond itself. To devote oneself to physical beauty was to neglect one's spiritual journey. But who cares about spiritual matters when you're a teenager trying to get a date? When Caoimhe was born, a friend sent us a children's storybook about a seed that grew into a twisted vine but produced no flowers. The seed wondered at its purpose. Then one night it bloomed, drenching the garden in a scent so strong it woke the old lady who had planted it. She wandered out into the garden in her nightie and was enraptured by the beauty of the vine's white flowers. I cannot do the book justice by reducing its themes to a sentence or two; I have made it sound sentimental and trite instead of sensitive and poignant. I doubt whether my girls understood its significance but the metaphor was not lost on Conor and me: the world is full of difference and true beauty is not always found in the obvious places. Still, I am saddened to think of Caoimhe shining in the dark, lonely garden, and me, grey and bent with old age, heaving my aching bones into action at her

summons, still there to praise and admire because no one
else will.

———

Perhaps I am alone in thinking like this; perhaps, like most of
the fears that stalk and maraud my head, it will evaporate like
dragon's breath once aired. Perhaps when Caoimhe is a
teenager I will look back on what I have written and laugh.
Maybe she will read it and laugh too. I suppose I have always
been fascinated by beauty, and struggled to make sense of it.
Take an ugly urban landscape and see it through the eyes of
an artist, or the ears of a musician and it can be transformed
into something spectacular. Does the magic of art create an
illusion of beauty or reveal what is truly there? I have no idea;
I can't seem to work it out. All I know is that I am flattened
by mass-productivity plainness. Barbie dolls and small plastic
toys are litter, and bring out my dark side. I like toys to be
made of wood or at least nothing synthetic. I make my own
dolls from outgrown baby clothes; they have odd-shaped arms
and lopsided plaits, but they are, I feel, more beautiful than
China's production line of impersonal plastic flawlessness.

   I suppose I love the idea of continuity, of connectedness.
When Caoimhe was born, people were afraid to find myself
or Conor in her. The braver souls who came to see us com-
mented on her hair, or skin colouring, but no one had the
nerve to say, 'She's got your chin.' It was impossible for people
to see beyond the hallmarks of disability. For a while
I struggled with it too. Then, when Caoimhe was almost two,
I remarked to a friend who had popped over that she was
looking more like me, and her reply was, 'Maybe, I suppose—

it's hard to tell.' Immediately I felt as though I had been doused in cold water. Over time, familiarity had blunted my awareness of her disability and this person's comment, harmlessly meant, put a boot in my nascent awareness. Conversely, it did point out to me how far I had come already along the path of acceptance. Once I had recovered from the shock of the diagnosis, it took time for Caoimhe's beauty to reveal itself again. Like a learner driver, I swerved from shrinking away from her features of Down syndrome to basking in her good looks. It was not easy to reconcile these two aspects of Caoimhe, the beauty and the beast.

That was then. As the months ploughed on, my new way of thinking became more embedded, more concrete, and now it's almost as natural as using two hands to play the piano. The moment of revelation came when Conor and I took what felt like quite a plunge, and went along to a Down's Syndrome Society open day. I spent the first half-hour adjusting to seeing such a high concentration of people with the syndrome in a world where you hardly see any. I had pushed through the gates into a different world, an invisible place, a sort of fairyland, or Narnia. After I adjusted, I could really look. I saw fat children, thin children, plain children, pretty children. I saw individuals, who looked like their parents, their sisters, their brothers; I saw normality. We left the venue as the sun melted and returning through the gate was like stepping into a different time zone, where we were oddities once more. We continued to take forays into this strange new world. Conor and I went to a charity function and sat on a table next to a family with several children. Over a lamb roast, I remarked to the father how much his youngest son, who had Down syndrome, looked like him and he recoiled as if shot. But it was true, the same spiky hair, the same pointy nose and inquisitive eyes. I burned with embarrassment.

When people remark on Caoimhe's looks I want to hug them. I want to thank them for seeing beyond the identifying hallmarks of disability to the girl within. Caoimhe thinks she is beautiful. She looks in the mirror, tries on a hat, grins and says 'pretty'. She has heard it from me a thousand times. Perhaps I am only reinforcing the message that looks matter, but what matters to me is that she knows I think she is beautiful.

Because she is. Her hair is the colour of honey, her eyes pale brown; she is rich and vibrant, like autumn. She looks like me and I am proud. But her beauty is not bound by physical constraints. When turbulent emotions rock my head I am soothed by her presence, like lying in a boat staring at the clouds. There is a vastness to her small self, endless as the sky. In her are embodied all the things I wish I could possess: charm, a delight in simplicity, unswerving trust, an ability to love without fear. I watch her as she potters around the playroom, pulling books from the shelves, flicking the pages, sing-song words fluttering from her lips, delicate as confetti. She picks up a book that makes her smile. She is heading towards me, waving it eagerly. As she comes closer, her steps quicken with purpose and she trips. She picks herself up, and resumes her trajectory like a programmed missile. I hold out my hand for the book; it is an old favourite, *Wheels on the Bus*. Its pages are splattered with garish ugly caricatures: mothers with yellow frizzy hair; fathers with big noses; ugly babies yelling. I meant to throw it out months ago but now it is too late, it has woven itself into the tapestry of her childhood. I lift her onto my lap and she chuckles and drums her legs back and forth with gleeful anticipation. She looks up at me with the shining confidence that I will turn this ugly thing into a work of beauty. I start to sing: 'The wheels on the bus . . .' and she joins in at the end of each line, whispering the word with quiet delight: 'Long!' When we have finished she throws her arms around my neck and clings for a second or two then draws back to stare at my face. She cups my cheeks in her starfish hands and wobbles my head. She touches my nose and pulls at my ears. She searches my features like a sculptor, chiselling, chipping away at the dull hardened surface, illuminating the beauty within. She pauses and stares; she likes what she sees. Her smooth face erupts into a smile and I am showered with stars.

Chapter 6
Nine Seconds

I read somewhere that it takes a child with Down syndrome, on average, nine seconds longer than other children to form a response to a question, an order, a sensation. In the raw weeks of early life, Caoimhe's responses were typical of any newborn. Her limbs jerked when brushed with cold air, and she would cry inexplicably, outrageously, her voice that of a stranger, loud and baffling, her mottled fists clenched in fury. I would rush to appease her, my movements spiked by anxiety because I did not yet know her; for nine months we had been intimate, but now we were like two foreigners trapped in a domestic farce. We would waltz uncomfortably around the sitting room, her screams getting louder, her face an exploding pomegranate of rage; I would lie her on her back, on her side, in her pram, in a hammock, pick her up, put her down; I would offer her milk which she ungraciously spewed back up over cushions and armchairs. Tiredness made me rodent-like and mechanical; I would pat, pace, rock, stroke in a mindless stupor, knowing I could only relax when she finally slept.

I struggled with the breastfeeding. I tried different positions on different chairs, but it was too often a frustrating, disappointing event. We latched together like ill-fitting apparel, uncomfortable and strained at the edges. I dreaded each session and so did she; her roar of dissatisfaction would eventually cause me to shrug her off, muttering darkly about bottles.

I hired a lactation consultant to come and witness our dismal duet. 'Down's babies usually sleep all the time,' she said, when I explained that my daughter simply couldn't—or at least not for more than twenty minutes at a stretch. She stared at Caoimhe's pinprick nostrils, crusted with the latest outpouring of her rage and confusion. 'They've always got cauliflowers up their noses, these kids,' she said, with an air of authority.

She prescribed dill weed for colic, and showed me in her brisk, know-all way how to put Caoimhe down to sleep, as if my other two children had not existed, or had been settled all their lives by some serene bedtime phantom and not my use-less self. My middle child was a great sleeper, I said weakly, defensively. 'Are you all right? You look ill,' was her response, as she peered at me through purple-painted eyes. 'Are you depressed?' 'Is she depressed?' she said, turning to Conor with-out waiting for my answer. She sat in our living room drinking tea while my daughter slept, peacefully, blissfully, maddeningly, for two hours. 'That's how you do it!' she exclaimed, as we finally managed to hustle her towards the door.

When Caoimhe was around five weeks old we began to understand one another. When I looked at her, her blank eyes would cloud with recognition. The corner of her lip jerked upwards, as if tugged by an invisible string. Her first smile was struggling to hatch. Over the days that followed, I watched it emerge, slowly, frustratingly. It would start in her eyes and work down the flat planes of her face until it reached the gash of her mouth and softened it. Sometimes it would conk out halfway down and I would be left feeling peculiarly deflated.

Her disability made urgent my need for that smile, that exquisite and long-awaited symbol of her love, breaking free from her sealed heart. It was in her smile I caught the first glimpses of her spirit, pure and mysterious and perfect, untouched by extra chromosomes. It healed the pain of her crying.

Once she discovered the value of a smile, she rarely stopped. The more she practised, the more adept she became—until it was only ever a second away. Then I missed watching its slow emergence that could halt me in my tracks, no matter how chaotic the day. I missed being sucked into her slow-motion life, instead of hurrying her through mine.

As the days passed, we stumbled into a rhythm; we began to fit back together. From her lips, the rest of her movements flowed downwards in a pattern predictable and punctual as chimes on a clock. Her limbs sprouted and stretched; her arms swiped the air, fists opening and closing like two small sea creatures. She kicked her legs and sucked her toes exactly according to the time scales in the baby manuals. She rolled from her front onto her back, then back the other way. At six months she was able to sit, and her world took on new dimensions. We would place her, legs bowed like a frog, in the middle of the playroom, surrounded by cushions, and her face would split into a delighted smile as she sat precariously, surveying her kingdom from her elevated plateau, before toppling like a drunk.

This new-found pleasure did not last long. The physiotherapist who visited every fortnight did not approve. Caoimhe had to learn to get into a sitting position herself, rather than having her parents arrange her like an ornament. We were given a regime of exercises to strengthen her muscles, which were to be performed on a mountain of foam shapes, borrowed from a toy library. I hated them, ugly things, in screaming gay orange or nerve-scraping blue, their vinyl surfaces scarred with pitted dirt, and bits of stuffing leaking at corners. They rose like technicoloured icebergs from a small sea of floor; after each session we seemed to acquire a new one, and so for a while our entire living space required careful navigation. I found myself unable to carry out the prescribed exercises, which required that a certain degree of force be applied; I did not have the mental strength to coerce Caoimhe into doing something which inevitably produced tears. So Conor took over the physio, working her reluctant limbs, gently, firmly, like a puppeteer. It would catch me in the throat to see the two of them on the floor together, him singing 'Hey de, hey de ho, the great big elephant is so slow,' as he bent her legs, pink and wobbly as blancmange, into a crawling action and manoeuvred her across a foam floor mat. During these sessions her thighs were shackled with two sweat bands sewn together by my own betraying hand, to stop them splaying to the sides. As she struggled along, she would cry with resentment and I cried too, but not in front of her. When she protested, I wore a mask of forced encouragement, a bright shiny smile, and my voice, artificial and high-pitched, churned out all the clichés from a safe distance: 'You can do it!' 'Almost there!' 'Nearly finished!' And she would look at me, look right through me, to the anxious ghost that hovered beneath, and cry.

At around twelve months she started to crawl. At first she levered herself up onto her arms and dragged the rest of her body around the room, like heavy baggage she'd been saddled with. Then she hoisted the lower half onto her knees. She would stare at herself, through the arch of her arms, fascinated with this levitation. She began to rock from side to side, then back and forth, puzzling at the mechanics of her own body. For a while it was as if she was torn between the security of my world and the seductive shimmer of her own; she was being pulled by opposing forces, for there was a small part of me that would silently whisper to her to stay, never leave. But then one day she was off, crawling away from me towards the mirage of independence, lured by a power that was stronger than maternal love. I watched her go, my pleasure curdled by tiny undercurrents of sorrow and loss.

———

Once she could crawl she set off every day, purposefully, like some ancient, determined explorer, to discover a new corner of the house. She discovered places I had yet to discover; her curiosity was unfettered and deadly. The caves of cupboards held great treasures: plastic bags, mouse traps, matches and marbles. But no cupboard gave her as much pleasure as her sisters' forbidden enclaves. They would come home from school to find their rooms rearranged, as if a poltergeist had taken up residence in their absence, and the walls would splinter with the decibels of their unified rage. Technology held special interest for Caoimhe, and her once soft pink fingers, now firmly probing and sticky, would find their way into all sorts of metal orifices. She had a magpie's love of silver and loved to watch our CDs wink and shine as they rolled across the floor.

She was vocal from an early age: 'ma–ma' and 'da–da', voiced somewhere around five or six months, were duly followed by 'ba–ba' and 'na–na'. Long chains of monotone sound would emerge from her lips, interrupted occasionally by a single jagged screech of delight at her ability. When she was a foetus, safely encased within me, I would play the piano—clumsily—hoping that through the tepid water the jar of wrong notes would be heard merely as a muted discord. When she was a newborn I would lie her in the pram next to the piano and hammer out my repertoire: 'Rock a Bye Baby', '*Eine Kleine Nacht musik*', 'Brahms Lullaby' and Simon and Garfunkel. For the first few months she lay as if in state, while I sang in a cracked voice and my fingers bulldozed the keyboard. At least she didn't cry. When she was a few months older I sat her on my lap while I played and she stared first at the music and then at my fingers, and her gaze would shift from one to another, blank with concentration. I believed that this would help her, that my ham-fisted music would give shape and form to the seeds of words buried inside her, so that one day they would rise easily from her lips, light and airy as dandelion clocks.

Baroque music is said to increase the number of synapses in the brain. Like extra bridges, synapses connect the various pathways criss-crossing the cortex, allowing more messages to get through, so I bought a pack of cut-price CDs to boost our limited collection. From then on, Bach's heavy, disciplined counterpoints filled the spaces between conversation in every room: we had Bach at breakfast, Bach at bath time, Bach at bedtime; 'Baching mad', mutters Conor cynically, quietly, under his breath.

Conor makes a living out of brains. In the first few years of Caoimhe's life, he was completing his doctorate in biomedical engineering, researching electroencephalography, or EEG. By attaching electrodes to the scalp, you can evaluate different functions of the brain by monitoring its electrical signals. The drawback is that it is unselective; like a badly tuned radio it picks up too many channels at once. Conor's research sought to discover ways of refining the process by cutting out some of the background interference. Every day he would pore over computer printouts of brainwave patterns, like some mad scientist. His desk was littered with photographs of volunteer test subjects—the balder, the better—with electrodes attached to their scalps and wafer-thin pages decorated with red and green peaks and troughs— crazy maps of someone's secret cerebral life. The aim, he explained bafflingly, was to synchronise the different coloured valleys and mountains. When an experiment worked, Conor would fizz and crackle with energy; when it didn't, he was flat and damp, as if all his charge had seeped out onto the crumpled page. The brain is the final frontier, he would tell me, the last unconquered recess of the human body. I love to think of its two spongy hemispheres, dark and bottomless as the universe, evading scientists' grabbing hands. But the human ego is indefatigable in its attempts to own and solve the transcendental mysteries of the mind.

Caoimhe has been born into a world preoccupied with brains. Her father grew up with the label 'bright', and by the time I met him, an engineer in his early twenties, he admitted to hating it, and wore it round his neck like a noose. The uncovering of his academic gifts at a young age had set him ticking on a trajectory from which, at times, he yearned to escape. Other talents he felt he may have had lay unseen in the shadow of this intellectual glare. While I had never particu-larly struggled at school, I grew up with the accepted under-standing that it was my brother, with his natural ability for maths, who was the clever one. My talents—artistic, creative—were more suited to hobbies than a career, it seemed. While my brother went to university, I merely went to art school. When I eventually became a journalist, after meandering through many tributaries of dried-up jobs, my father, a former sub-editor, told me to work on magazines. Newspapers, he warned, were tough places, men's domain. Even now, despite more than a decade of working for the press, and winning awards for my writing, I still think of my brother as the clever one.

———

When my first two children came along I could see that they were quick-witted and sharp as new teeth. I took their natural intelligence for granted and never filled the house with vulgar plastic toys passed off as 'early learning'; I left them to play with their own imaginations. Conor and I both took the mistakes of a previous generation and made different ones. Neither of us are pushy parents. When the ring of school interrupted childhood, we chose a Waldorf education, based on the philosophies of the Austrian mystic Rudolf Steiner, for our girls. This type of schooling is not in abundance; we drove through a desert of suburbs to get to the nearest venue, with the girls bored and fighting in the back of the car. Our more conventional friends and family saw our choice as radical, even irresponsible: in Steiner schools children don't learn to read until the age of eight; there is virtually no competitiveness and a strong emphasis is placed on creative learning and music. It required much steely resolve from us

not to cave in when we saw our children's contemporaries en-
grossed in Harry Potter while ours still couldn't read road
signs. But at least they were able to knit and paint and amuse
themselves from an early age without the need of plastic
props, and they could relax, at least most of the time, without
the anaesthesia of television. Of course, you never know
if you've done the right thing until your kids hit 40: then, if
they're not in therapy, or prison, and are able to read, perhaps
you did okay. So it remains to be seen.

Anyway, Wynnie had just started kindergarten, and Ellie
was halfway through year two, when Caoimhe landed like a
cuckoo in the middle of our smug cerebral nest. With her
arrival, all my insecurities about intelligence lay ugly and
exposed. I was soon filling the house with brightly coloured
squishy rattles that pinged and buzzed like microwave ovens
and mobiles that played canned lullabies. Previously shunned
plastic toys with labels that boasted of improving motor,
sensory or intellectual skills littered the floor and oozed from
closed cupboards. I went through a phase of believing every
moment in Caoimhe's life had to be a learning opportunity
or else it was wasted, and I'd contort myself in an effort to
make it so. I'd chat to her endlessly about my day, telling
her what I was doing in bright primary vernacular: Look
Caoimhe! Mammy's baking a cake! Here's an egg! Look! I'm
cracking the egg! Look Caoimhe! Mammy's cracking up!'

For a time it felt like I was. Like a muddled mathematician
I'd pore over the equation that was everyone's needs,
but I could never get it to balance. Someone always went
short. I remember overhearing Wynnie saying sadly to
herself, 'Mammy only likes babies', and I felt that serrated
knife of guilt twist another inch. Meanwhile Caoimhe would

watch me, her all-singing, all-dancing mother, from her highchair, head slightly cocked to one side, gentle eyes quizzical, prob-ably thinking: 'Why can't she just shut up?'

My voracious reading about Down syndrome in the first bleak weeks after Caoimhe's diagnosis had left me confused about the importance of early intervention for children with intellectual disability. Some texts argued that children with Down's learn best in the first few years of life, their ability to learn decelerating with age. Targeted programmes run by experts were the best way of helping Caoimhe, these books suggested. Reading them, I'd feel the thorns of inadequacy pricking; I was not doing enough. And then I'd remember other books which sighed at the mere mention of inter-vention and wearily concluded that there was no convincing evidence that intensive therapy allowed children with Down syndrome to learn any faster.

———

So did it make a difference or didn't it? Cautiously, I joined up Caoimhe to a playgroup for children with special needs. We turned up on a Monday morning, me as nervous as if it were my first day at school. The playgroup was held in a building on a street specialising in the medically misshapen: farther down were plastic surgeons, ear nose and throat specialists and eye doctors. In a large sunny room flanked by ominous foam shapes sat a circle of mothers with their children, all under five. The circle bulged outwards as a space was made for the cumbersome cluster that was myself, my daughter (attached to me tight as a barnacle), a pram and a bag containing the hated towelling shackles. The playgroup leader, a jolly woman, turned towards us and sang a welcome with her guitar: 'Hello to you Caoimhe! Hello to you Caoimhe! Hello hello hello hello hello to you Caoimhe!' Everyone in the group turned and waved at her, smiling. Instinctively my daughter buried her face deeper in my clothing and we clung to one another for support. It was an animated world we had entered, where facial expressions were an outrageous fashion accessory, like hats at Ascot. One didn't just say a word, any word; each letter had to be vocally enhanced and accompanied by a mad hand gesture. In this circus of language our eyebrows shot up and outwards, our eyes artificially wide, our mouths stretched unnaturally around words we were used to taking short cuts with—the sheer effort would stimulate a fit of yawning. A basket of instruments was passed around. Caoimhe took a set of bells and shook them tentatively. She put them in her mouth, enjoying the taste of cool chunky metal, and they were immediately whisked away, contaminated. We sang a song about frogs, and I, along with the other mothers, squatted and jumped like inmates at Bedlam while Caoimhe stared, unreadable, silent. A child trying to crawl away bumped her head and howled; the injury was immediately noted and recorded. After the singing, the speech therapist appeared with an enormous book which contained cartoon-like drawings of cats composed of thin black lines, excessively pointed whiskers and claws like railway arches. They bore little resemblance to any living animal I have ever seen. We learnt sign language for cat; I had to stroke my hand as if it were a friendly feline. At the end of the book we wiggled our thumbs at our children to show them it had finished.

I felt remarkably self-conscious, like a foreign language student. I never took to signing. My communication with Caoimhe until this point had been through words, touch, or just something invisible, intangible. Now I was wagging my thumb ferociously at her, and stroking my hand, pretending it was a cat. I felt daft. What's more, she knew I felt daft. In company, I would sign furtively, surreptitiously, as if the two of us were involved in some cloak-and-dagger operation, some form of espionage. Eventually, quietly, I gave up on signing. Now only the remnants of our early crude communication remain; I still wiggle my thumb when she has finished eating, and she grins and wiggles hers back—a shared memory of our awkward experience.

I went back to the playgroup again and again, finding a gap in the circle, edging my way awkwardly in. I don't know what drew me back; I looked forward to these Monday sessions with as much enthusiasm as I remember I used to have for a double physics class. On the surface it was not much different from a regular playgroup, if you ignored the feeding tubes, the leg braces and the splints. But to me, the group, the ring, was a symbol of the world I had entered; where smiles and exaggerated kindness were buttered thickly over the dark chasms of untidy emotions. Nobody cried, no one looked fed up, or as if they had been lying awake all night, fighting off the future. Neither did I. I fished out my smile from the bottom of my bag, where it lay among the terry towelling shackles, before I entered the room, and took it off in the car when I was a safe distance away, with a small sigh of relief, as though I was kicking off a pair of pinching winklepickers.

I went back because I wanted to belong somewhere. I no longer fitted in the world of normality; as a mother and child we had been marked from birth. But I didn't feel I belonged here either, among the walking frames, the specially adapted feeding chairs and the butterfly-bright conversation. While I felt deep gratitude towards the therapists who could do this work, who recognised the value of a life that would once have been deemed worthless, my guilt at not wholly embracing the experience, at digging under the surface with prying hands, made me feel more isolated.

This was not what we needed. Caoimhe was simply not disabled enough. After a bit of hunting around, we found two new playgroups: one was a Steiner one, where she and her peers ate soup from wooden bowls and played with cloth dolls, and the other was specifically for children with Down's, where the toys were bright and functional, and designed to improve skills.

Now we belonged to both worlds.

Shortly after Caoimhe's first birthday, new words started to emerge. After mammy and daddy came 'oof' for a dog, then 'moo' for a cow, and soon there was an entire farmyard in our house; at times, cross-bred like evil genetic experiments, pigs would quack and horses baa, and once a monkey with a strange demonic laugh moved in. Caoimhe learnt to name bits of her body and could point with authority to her nose, my nose, strangers' noses, her tummy, chin and toes. In no time at all she had an artillery of words which she fired like lethal bullets: Book! Read! Cake! Eat!

Her physical development continued as preordained by some greater force, despite my lack of enthusiasm for physio. After a few months of crawling she became a bi-ped, swaying giddily on sapling limbs, blown by an invisible wind from chair to sofa to table. Her gait was stiff; she did not lift her unblemished knees and carefully plant each step like other toddlers. Instead, she moved like a scarecrow, like some wind-up toy, her joints braced for support, her arms raised high, as if still hanging on to heaven.

———

By two she knew her colours and her world lit up. She would point at various objects and say with wonder: 'Boo!' 'Wed!' 'Gween!' 'Yellow' was always uttered lovingly, the final syllable exhaled in a long breathy sigh. She was walking well now, but she tired easily; her short limbs kept her in clothes for one-year-olds and her lack of balance made her precarious. Shortly after her second birthday, we finally left Australia and moved to Northern Ireland—to a house with stairs which delighted her, but kept me in a state of chronic anxiety every time I watched her wobble down them. (The uncertainty of our life in Melbourne, which I mentioned in Chapter Two, hadn't disappeared. In fact, debating this small life event— ha!—formed the backdrop to our conversations after Caoimhe's birth. The possibility of returning would afflict our thoughts, our sentences, like a mental tic. Our inability to make a decision about the future became a handicap in its own right. In the end the decision was more or less made for us—but more of that in Chapter Nine.)

For those first few months in this strange new place we lived in a cocoon, seeing no one, apart from the neighbours: no therapists, doctors or maternal health nurses—the scaffolds of Caoimhe's life in Australia. We emerged from a long, shapeless summer and joined a local playgroup and suddenly I was surrounded by other two-year-olds and I was shocked: Caoimhe appeared so fragile, so baby-like, next to their solidness. I watched a robust boy the same age as her climb and swing from a chair; bite into an apple; go down a slide: all things that Caoimhe couldn't do and I was alarmed. I phoned the local health nurse to inquire about disability services and she said we would need a referral from a developmental paediatrician. She contacted someone on our behalf and I waited for the letter to come; it didn't. I phoned up to discover there was a five-month delay.

I went on an internal rampage, railing against an inadequate, faceless health service that made a mockery of the term 'early intervention'. When I had finished raging, I picked up the phone, and with the help of the health nurse obtained an appointment two months down the line. This, I felt, was a victory.

It is a hollow one, though, because really I still have no idea if therapy works. Sometimes I wonder, uneasily, if it is more about helping me than Caoimhe, by making her more acceptable to a critical society and giving me something to focus on. I had no say in creating a child like Caoimhe but I can control, or at least influence, to some extent, how she turns out. The truth is that while society may be tolerant of children like Caoimhe, nobody wants them. She has been born into a world stained by intellect, where she is considered less important than the doctors and scientists whose medical breakthroughs allow her to enjoy a longer and healthier life in a world where she is not valued.

———

There is plenty of evidence of this. In 2004, the UK's Down's Syndrome Association carried out a major survey, examining the barriers that exist to providing good education for children with the condition. It found that 32 per cent of parents had experienced discrimination and prejudice from education professionals. One parent reported how a head teacher had summed up children with Down syndrome, saying 'some of them can be quite violent, can't they?' Another principal told a parent: 'We have good grades here. That won't continue if your daughter comes here.'

This obsession with intelligence begins in foetal life, when the baby's developing brain, its precious jewel, is jealously guarded by its parents. The newspapers run regular stories about how to boost brain function; mothers are told the best foods to eat for embryonic brain development and advised to avoid stress, which can harm the foetal brain. When her child is eventually born, the mother is encouraged to breastfeed, because babies reared on their mother's milk are cleverer than bottle-fed ones.

The baby's first year of life is cluttered with props to catapult her to intellectual greatness. There are Baby Einstein books containing baffling pictures of blue goats and purple zebras; there are electronic toys to teach a child of one to be bilingual. According to *The Observer*, in 2004 parents in the UK spent £2 billion on toys for preschool children in an attempt to immunise them from the disease of mediocrity. In May 2006, *The Guardian* reported that along with Baby Einstein, rival companies like Brainy Baby have generated $1 billion in sales in the US since their launch in the mid-nineties.

The Baby Einstein range, targeted at under-twos, features

great figures from science and the arts: titles include Baby
Bach, Baby Newton and Baby Mozart Music Festival. Baby
Wordsworth 'will foster the development of your toddler's
speech and language skills'. Brainy Baby claims its *Peek-a-Boo*
video is 'brain stimulating' and will help 'nurture such
important skills as . . . cause and effect and language development'. Apparently, 49 per cent of American parents believe that
plonking their babies down in front of a TV screen showing
technicoloured zoo animals playing instruments and behaving
like humans is important in their children's education.

Recently a group led by a Harvard psychologist filed a
complaint with the federal trade commission arguing that
advertisements for the videos in the US are deceptive because
there is no evidence that watching them helps babies learn.
Here is the baby, fully formed but empty, waiting to be filled
with bits and scraps of knowledge, information, facts, foods,
supplements, stimulants, sounds, words and pictures. When,
as a toddler, she counts to three, echoing meaningless sounds
plucked from the continuous fug around her, her parents clap
delightedly and call her clever.

Everyone wants a child with a high IQ, and some parents
will go to questionable lengths to make it happen. During our
first summer in Northern Ireland I read an article about a
local woman who ditched her partner and trawled the net to
find better-quality sperm to father her offspring: 'Could
I find someone younger, taller, more athletic-looking and
mathematically gifted—but who also wasn't "real" and
therefore wouldn't shoot icy stares at me across the dinner
table?'

She scrutinised the available advertised donors with the
same sort of detachment as a customer buying white goods.

'Ordering the father of my child on a website was especially difficult for me because I am not a good online shopper,' she told us breezily. She took to calling the receptionist at the fertility clinic where the men deposited their wares for detail on the curl of hair, the size of biceps, and concluded: 'The second you separate mating from dating it's okay to indulge hubristic fantasies of genetic engineering.' There was a short wait for her chosen sperm to become available, and she was pregnant on the second attempt. It was at that point I hated her. I had wanted her to fail, to be denied the short cut to a supposed perfection she obviously craved; that I had craved, too, but had been denied.

Despite her success, the woman bemoaned her situation: she didn't choose to be a single mother; it was the fault of the era in which she grew up, the Generation X slackers. 'Unlike women a decade or two older we took it for granted we could do anything we wanted—which explains why a lot of us became paralysed by indecision.' I am from the same generation but I do not feel paralysed by indecision, only weary with the relentless pressure to acquire knowledge that will make me richer, cleverer, more powerful. Like greedy children, our generation has been urged to stretch out our hands and grasp what we want; by taking it we can possess it too. But my hands are tired of grasping, because I am surrounded, bombarded. I cannot shop in a supermarket these days without emerging feeling battered by choice. Our material knowledge has no doubt increased, but I wonder about wisdom.

While I realise this on a conscious level, the message has yet to fully penetrate my soul, where I still mourn for my perfect child, the one who would have gone to Oxford. After

Caoimhe was born I found myself doing IQ tests late at night
at the computer. It was as if I had to prove something to
myself, that her birth had not stolen something from me, that
I was still intelligent. Oh the irony, to be sitting in front of a
computer in a dressing gown and carpet slippers at midnight,
trying to work out, through a fog of tiredness, the correct
combination of legs belonging to nine chickens, two dogs and
three cats in less than twenty seconds. Up until her birth I had
been a successful journalist; now I was a nobody, the mother
of a disabled child, with no real hope of pursuing my career.
I felt my life was held hostage by hers; the glitter of any future
career must tarnish so that hers could sparkle. Our symbiosis
would continue into her adulthood; we would never really be
separate. I saw myself grey and bent, driving her to functions,
cooking her meals, accompanying her on dates to the cinema,
sitting in the back row, her constant shadowy chaperone.

Her rewards will become my rewards, usurping the ones I
would have got on my own merit, if only I had the time. I am
already seeing the evidence. At the age of two years and four
months, Caoimhe's development still fits within a normal
range. She walks and talks, eats and—occasionally, obligingly
—uses a potty. If I give up my job, and continue to prune and
trim my hours so that I can extract another few minutes to
spend with her, she may cruise this trajectory for years to come.
The thought tosses around my head like a restless sleeper; it
niggles at moments I steal for myself, like some adulterous
lover, tainting the experience with guilt. I read furtively,
secretly, in hidden locations for minutes at a time: Carl Jung
on the toilet, Ian McEwan in the bath, *Hello!* in car parks.
I look back and marvel at my twenties, at time blissfully
squan-dered, ignorant of what lurked around the corner.

And the pay-off for my labour brings its own peculiar poignancy: Caoimhe will come to recognise and struggle with her own difference, will come to understand what she will never be, will compare herself to her sisters and weep. In some ways it would be easier if she was too disabled to notice.

It is a futile race I am running. Gradually I will notice her slowing down, lagging behind. At some point she will leave the path of her contemporaries and join a different one, frequented by spectres we have yet to meet. I do not know at which point this will happen—in childhood, in adolescence, or in adulthood, when the first lesions of the dreaded Alzheimer's may start to coat her brain like rust.

In those early months, when I swung between acceptance and denial, I collected scraps of stories, wisps of myth, holding on to them as if they were concrete, tangible facts. Someone knew of somebody at a university where one of the lecturers had Down syndrome! Someone knew of someone with Down's who had a baby! Someone knew of someone with Down's who lived to be eighty! Shock made an idiot of me, while hope charged me with energy; after the children had gone to bed, I would trawl the Internet for treatments that could soften the blow of Caoimhe's diagnosis. She could be injected with freeze-dried cells from cattle or sheep which would migrate to corresponding organs in her body and revitalise them! (Though studies show the only statistical difference was that treated children had better hair.) This type of therapy is now banned in most countries, because of the risk of triggering Creutzfeldt-Jakob disease—and not because it is simply madness to take a child and inject it with animal parts to make it more acceptable to society.

By the end of her first month I knew an awful lot about my

daughter's unusual brain chemistry. Thanks to some unfortu-
nate mice enlisted for use in a transgenic experiment, I know
that it is a gene with the acronym DYRK that causes her brain
to struggle with learning. I know how the presence of this
extra genetic material floods her system with an overdose of
enzymes and how her body battles to mop them up; how extra
antioxidants, vitamins A, C and E, beta-carotene, coenzyme
Q and the minerals zinc and selenium could help soak up this
excess. One article that I read likened her to a cake recipe with
too many ingredients: the imbalance having to be rectified
by nutrition.

I bought a punnet of blueberries, each velvet orb a powerhouse of antioxidants. I put one in front of Caoimhe.
'Blueberry,' I said. 'Boo bee,' she replied, staring at it with
fascination. After rolling it around for a while, she picked it
up gingerly between finger and thumb and put it in her
mouth. She chewed it slowly, and then reached for the punnet
and picked up another, and then another, gathering
momentum.

When she had eaten the whole punnet she screamed for
more—'More boo bee!'—on that day developing an expensive blueberry habit. Soon we were going through two
punnets a day. One Sunday in late summer we drove for
almost two hours to a blueberry farm set in a valley of yellow
Australian bush and bought four kilos. Two weeks later they
were gone. The farm had closed for the season, but an
arrangement was made; I could pick up a package left on the
doorstep. Once more we made the journey in the searing heat
and Caoimhe ate blueberries all the way home, her mouth
drooling juice like vampire blood. It would have been easier
to buy her a supplement.

You could fill a barn with the arguments and counter-arguments about what is known as Targeted Nutritional Intervention, or various ways to lessen the impact of Down syndrome by administering mega-doses of vitamins and minerals. Proponents, namely parents and manufacturers, claim that TNI, as it is snappily abbreviated, can increase IQ and reduce health problems, whereas its detractors, mainly doctors, say it can't. Figures and formulas are spouted, lobbed and deflected across cyberspace like hand grenades.

Dr Langdon Down has made a science of my child and left her open to exploitation and heated argument. I have dulled my brain trying to decipher what is genuine and what is sinister capitalisation, to sift through the mountain of straw, and am no closer to the truth. There is no miller's daughter who will come along and spin it into gold. Vulnerable parents will look in dark places in an attempt to heal their wounds. I even came across a product which purports to change the appearance of children with Down's, the company's website boasting before and after photographs of a twelve-year-old girl who had been taking the formula for two years. I puzzled over the pictures. Like the child in 'The Emperor's New Clothes', I couldn't see the difference: yes, she was slimmer and had shed some puppy fat; her hair had grown; her teeth had been straightened, but her eyes, screwed up to avoid the sun, had not lost their almond shape.

How can taking a potion alter the blueprint of a face, a nose, the eyes? I imagined feeding a cocktail of enzymes to Caoimhe, seeing her face slowly melt and harden into something different, watching her seal-pup eyes straighten, the smooth bump of her nose elongate, and I shuddered. It felt creepy, like bad science fiction, to alter someone's basic structure, other than in fantasy.

In a pharmacy in Belfast, Conor picks up a leaflet of a bright-eyed child holding a placard advertising fish oil. Apparently in a trial carried out by an English education authority, it had been shown to improve behaviour and short-term auditory memory. I give Caoimhe a teaspoon of fish oil; she wrinkles her nose and it drools down her chin, leaving a puddle of wasted intelligence on the floor. I buy a tin of sardines instead. 'Fish!' I say, and show her the sardines, embalmed with oil in their metal casket. She looks at them dubiously and goes over to our goldfish, swimming disconsolately in their plastic tank. 'Fish!' she says. She has made the connection and will not eat them.

Every day I marvel at my daughter's intelligence. I wonder how, not so very long ago, children with Down syndrome were deemed uneducable and therefore not entitled to schooling. In this way I am paradoxically grateful that those with learning disabilities have been caught up in the academic heatwave that has gripped our climate.

I discover another article, written by a neuroscientist and father of a girl who has the condition. He argues, strongly, convincingly, that Down syndrome must be seen as a disease, a slow and creeping one that over the years deprives the sufferer of their mental faculties. He bemoans the lack of research into drug therapies, compared with rarer conditions such as Rett syndrome or Fragile X syndrome, and laments the prevailing attitude that insists the condition is immutable, simply a variation of the typical human experience. He quotes Dr Jérôme Lejeune, the French doctor who discovered that Down syndrome was caused by the presence of an extra chromosome, and who described the condition as 'an implacable disorder depriving the children of the most precious quality afforded by our genetic patrimony, the full power of rational thinking'.

I look at my daughter and try to see her as disabled, diseased, but I cannot. I try to galvanise myself into action; I should be seeking out formulas and supplements that can 'normalise' her. But I can only see through her, to something mysterious underneath, to something gleaming with health, so pure, so pristine, that I cannot bear to tamper with it, and would not take the risk. Is the ability to think rationally really our most precious quality? I feel dampened by the thought.

Shortly after she was born, I developed an infection and visited a GP. After prescribing antibiotics she looked at my sleeping daughter and said, 'Really, it's not so different having a child with Down's. They're very loving children, but they can act inappropriately. They're just not very bright.' She mentioned a list of jobs my child might be capable of doing in eighteen years time: factory work, sheltered workshop work, gardening. Meanwhile Caoimhe slept, curled up in her capsule, a pearl in a plastic shell—her smile, her secret weapon, her invaluable currency, safely stored away.

I believe the doctor is wrong, that my daughter is starbright, not yet dulled by intellectualism, by academic failure, by performance anxiety, by attitudes like hers. Caoimhe is illuminated with a radiance of being, of recognising and finding joy in a moment lost on those worn down by knowledge. People who are not primed to become great intellectual achievers can bring something else to this world, to an unbalanced society. My daughter has an innate understanding of the human condition; she was an early connoisseur of emotion. As a baby, if a child cried within her presence, she would cry too, covering her face with her hands, curling into a ball; the child's sadness almost too much for her to bear. Now she is older, she has lost some of that intensity and is able to put some distance between herself and the distressed, but will still point at a sobbing child, will recognise its sadness and acknowledge it in sombre tones. The idea that we can only understand the world through intellect is a false one, and a life lived as such is only half a life. The gifts of the heart are as vital to society as those of the head; in Caoimhe's short life she has changed mine immeasurably. I teach her the rudiments of intellectual thinking; she teaches me the ways of the spirit, gives me wisdom—and so we complement each other perfectly.

I fear that my daughter will become flattened by the relentless intellectual juggernaut that shoves its way, like a bad-taste housing developer, into the magical, mysterious landscape of childhood in an attempt to create something newer, better, shinier. I fear that she will emerge from her garden only to be judged an academic failure, a lesser being, her self-esteem shrunken like a midday shadow. And so my job, as I see it, is not to stuff her with knowledge but to shield her from its oppressiveness; to give her the gift of an ordinary life, not one burdened by an intellectual overload, to protect what is in danger of being crushed—the spirit that connects her with us as equals, if we let it.

Chapter 7
Pretend You're the Mother

People often ask me how my three daughters get on together. It's a fair question, considering the lingering belief that having a child with a disability will somehow be a millstone, a lifelong burden for those happy, healthy brothers and sisters who would otherwise have skipped through life without ever being hampered by anyone else's neediness. But excuse me while I rinse and spit that mouthful of sarcasm.

Of course I had concerns, initially, built on ignorance, outdated data and a continuing poor public image of disability (a black word with shades of grey) that weaves among us, like an invisible snake spreading its venom, and holds that a person with a learning disability is a lesser being, a thing to be feared, even eradicated. But now, two and a half years down the track, I can honestly say that I do not have such big concerns in this department.

———

Since Caoimhe's birth, I have applied organic farming methods to sowing the seeds of sibling love. I have nurtured the girls' relationship from the earliest of days and I am confident of getting good results. I have invested enormous amounts of energy into molecular bonding; Jesus, I have virtually welded them together with a blow-torch. And for the moment the girls love each other. Everyone remarks on it. Ellie, in particular, adores her small and annoying sister, who, in turn, sees her in a halo of golden light. They hug, play, shout, scream, like normal sisters. As I write, they are in the playroom; Ellie is a queen (as always) and Wynnie and Caoimhe her minions. Caoimhe, a particularly rebellious underling, is wrapped in swathes of coloured cloth that her short legs continually trip over (good physio, I think). She will not take orders from the queen but runs, giggling, to the kitchen, chased by someone in a royal rage. Wynnie is always a faithful minion, dutiful and obeying, while secretly dreaming of killing the queen, or at least dethroning her and stealing her power. (Wynnie gets the second-best dress-ups.) This vignette, so Enid Blytonly-ordinary, assures me that all is well. Then again, I could be deluding myself, as in any aspect of parenting. Perhaps I am running like a cartoon character, and if I actually look down I will see that I have gone over the edge of the cliff, my legs rotating madly in a whoosh of fresh air. The truth is I will not know until my girls become parents themselves how they really feel about having a sister with a disability, or what sort of a job I did helping them to deal with her birth. When you deliver a child, you deliver a past, a secret magpie's nest of oddments and scraps of feeling—sensations left over from childhood, collected and stored, but not understood; wrenched from their hiding place and dragged into the light by the emerging foetus. Nothing is more self-revealing than becoming a mother. So who knows?

Perhaps when I am dead they will put Caoimhe in a home and my mantle of smugness will be ripped from my hollow skeleton.

———

After Caoimhe was born, guilt buzzed around my brain like flies around a doggy deposit. There was this ugly thing which sat, brown and squat, next to the dazzling miracle of her birth, an unpleasant, untouchable thing, which I kept covered with a silk cloth, waiting for the right moment to reveal it to my unsuspecting audience. Da da! Like the turn of a kaleidoscope, Caoimhe's diagnosis had altered the composition of my world but I was loath to alter Ellie's and Wynnie's. In their world, according to the fairy tales they feasted on, disability didn't exist amongst the beautiful and the good; it belonged to the plain, the unbecoming, the unintelligent—amphibians, trolls or gnomes, usually. In fantasy there are no grey areas; the world is a neat dichotomy of good and bad. Caiomhe was a princess, but one word from me and this shining, heavenly being would turn into a cumbersome frog. And so I said nothing. Partly because I was still soft as a bruise, unable to summon the courage, and partly because I wanted the girls to get to know her, to love her for what she was, before turning her into a millstone, an albatross, like the one in Coleridge's foreboding poem 'The Rime of the Ancient Mariner', which they would have to carry the rest of their lives. We lived in this strange hiatus for maybe six weeks or so, a chasm between my world and theirs, created by my secret of knowing. During this time I observed my children differently, detachedly, as if they were not mine but someone else's. I admired their beauty, their wellness, their strength, and felt such a sentimental gratitude for their sheer perfection that it could cause tears to spring up at inopportune moments. I wondered how I had taken their births so much for granted; their robust development. I don't think for a minute I had imagined what my life would be like if they were born with a disability. I was possessed of a brazen confidence that expected them to be beautiful and clever, and they were. I realise now that they are my pride and joy, the success that partly fills the hollow of my failure. This realisation is, in difficult times, the boiler-house fire that keeps me going.

Every day I wondered how to tell them about their sister. I had many hypothetical scenarios and imaginary conversations. I was determined not to cry, to find the right tone: serious but not threatening; concerned but not panicky; factual but coloured with delicate shades of emotion. I didn't air my thoughts; they buzzed around my head like trapped flies. Conor, a pragmatic man, concentrated on getting to the appointments on time, organising finances, keeping the mechanics of our life well oiled. I do not have a practical nature and so I saw it as my job to look after the emotional side of things. We slipped into our prescribed roles that had been the success of our union so far.

Looking back, it is clear that Conor and I did reach some sort of mutual agreement not to tell the girls immediately, in those raw weeks when my voice was liable to collapse midsentence; to wait until we were stronger, so that we could talk evenly, answer questions, without falling apart. We both knew that we wanted Ellie and Wynnie to get to know Caoimhe slowly, to love her as a baby, not hate her as a problem, before we threw the punch. Yet neither of us can remember openly discussing the best time to tell them; there is no 'tonight's the night' memory seared on my brain. We each felt our way, slowly, cautiously, as if navigating a sheer rock face; conversation felt extraneous and difficult; we found other ways to communicate.

In the end, I brought it up over dinner. Rotating a piece of chicken around my plate with a nervous monotony, I explained about difference. Ellie can't eat gluten; Wynnie has what we call a 'star' eye, a mix of blue and brown. Caoimhe has an extra chromosome. 'She'll do everything that you do, only slower,' I said clumsily, helping myself to another tomato. It was a few weeks before I realised that they'd completely misunderstood. They thought Caoimhe would move slowly, like a spaceman on the moon. They'd envisaged waiting for her for endless minutes while she planted each leg in front of the other; imagined her sentences lost in infinity as the words came out like a tape recorder on slow batteries. The relief they felt when I explained it again, better, was comic. 'Oh, is that all?' was their general attitude. What was epochal for me, was, I realised, a non-event for them.

———

Saying that, the early weeks were hard on the girls, especially Wynnie, who had lost her place as the baby in the family. Caoimhe's appointments took up endless hours, and Conor and I were so scared about being apart when news was given that we always attended them together, the three of us a tense, defensive troika. Our insistence on being together meant off-loading the children onto various friends. Wynnie made sure this desertion of duty was atoned for. She regressed to the sort of babyish behaviour which resulted in instant attention for Caoimhe, but an impatient rolling of the parental eyes when she did it. She found a dummy in a drawer and started sucking on it. Once, I found her dressed in her old baby clothes which she'd rifled from a storage chest. A top meant for a six-month-old, garnished with scarlet ladybirds, strained across her midriff, the insects' smiling faces contorted into grimaces, her arms asphyxiated by sleeves which had given up their difficult journey at the elbows. The trousers pulled taut across her thighs reminded me of a desperate American housewife. Wynnie spent the best part of a week parading around in this get-up, outrageous and poignant as a drag artist, with the dummy drooping from her mouth like a fag. Whether she was reclaiming herself as the displaced baby, or her emotional antennae, vibrating softly, invisibly, as hummingbird's wings, were responding to my sadness at my imperfect baby by offering herself up as the perfect one, I am not sure. But when I caught sight of her my heart would flatten with the weight of my guilt. Ellie was buffered from this emotional maelstrom by school; meanwhile Wynnie thrashed about in the thick of it, like a last-gasp mackerel on the deck. Grief and shock blinded me to just how much she was suffering. I was polarised by frenzied periods of activity—of cleaning, cooking, being seen to be coping—and a paralysis that froze my brain like a computer virus. Neither mother was much use to her. The epiphany came one day when I was rushing around like a whirling dervish, cleaning, picking up a jumble of old socks, fir cones and pieces of jigsaw, before some visitor with a clipboard was due to descend. 'Can we play?' asked Wynnie, appearing in front of me, blocking the doorway. 'What shall we play?' say I, irritably, looking like the Cat in the Hat's Cleaning Machine, with various objects wedged under my arm, or balanced precariously, as I tried to dodge around her. 'Pretend you're the mother,' says my daughter, and I stop in my tracks. Pretend I'm the mother? What do you mean, pretend? I am your effing mother . . . aren't I?

I look at my daughter, her speckled face and her dark gypsy curls, and I really look. I see a small child who is not my child; she is older than the one I had when I last really looked. There is a defiance about her which has hardened her edges, an anger that has stolen her baby-ness. She stares at me and I stare back at her and the air around us is a soup of sadness and longing. I put down the heap of clutter. 'I don't know what to do,' I say lamely, and she produces a pair of high heels and a hat with dried dusty flowers and I put it on, aware that I am a pathetic spectacle, a circus clown, being humoured by its child audience. She passes me a shiny black handbag with a tarnished clasp and a rip in its patent leather and I clutch it to myself for protection.

Wynnie did not take to having a baby sister. Before I became pregnant she and I enjoyed an easy relationship. As a baby she ate well and slept well, those things so dear to a mother's heart. There were none of the health problems I had with Ellie, or the teething problems I had with first-time motherhood, just a sort of easiness which made spending time with her pleasant and fun—and so I did a lot of it. We drifted in and out of each other's worlds as if passing from one room to another; she was happy to help while I cooked, sitting on the floor with a pan and a wooden spoon, and I enjoyed being the guest of honour at her dolls' tea party, or a customer in her shop. In the summer we'd go walking and look for dolphins in the bay, a hard-wearing 24-carat delight for a person who grew up on a housing estate in the north of England. Wynnie was born on a warm spring day and warmth seemed to ooze into all corners of her babyhood. Her first two years were as comforting and uneventful as white noise; there were no jarring spikes or shudders of drama or calamity; no biblical-style demonic tantrums or late-night hospital visits. The only time she got sick was when we went on holiday; the rude interruption to her predictable routine sent her body reeling.

As early as I can remember, Wynnie was in awe of her big sister, three years her senior, and imitated her every move. When Ellie drew a horse, she would try to draw one too, poring over the page, sneaking a glance at her sister's (fiercely protected by a wall of arm), then crumpling in disappointment at what she produced. She wanted to play with Ellie's friends; when they rode bikes up and down the drive, she followed on her trike, legs pedalling like mad windmill sails in an attempt to keep up. And when they finally left her, shutting the bedroom door firmly behind them, laughter seeping underneath like toxic gas, she would bellow. I felt the hurt of her exclusion like a phantom pain; perhaps I went a bit overboard in trying to mop up all those sad feelings that registered in her heaving shoulders and red eyes. When Ellie was at pre-school I would devote my energy to Wynnie, stockpiling her with love against future distress.

And then I got pregnant. Sickness held me captive for the entire length of my pregnancy; in Wynnie's eyes, our games petered to a halt and I became a new sort of mother, attempting to play from a horizontal position, puncturing our games with bouts of throwing up. I lived for the two days she went to childcare and I could be sick unencumbered by guilt. Sometimes I would wake from a doze on a couch to find her staring at me, her eyes level, her face sombre and impenetrable, like Wednesday Addams. I didn't know what to tell her. If I told her I was to have another baby in six months' time, would she hate the baby for making her mother sick? If I didn't tell her, would she hate me? I can't remember what I chose to do; when I look back to that time, all I can see is her eyes staring at me—dark, defiant, betrayed.

———

On the morning after Caoimhe's birth, before we were given the diagnosis, Wynnie hid behind a chair rather than be photographed with her unwanted sister. The baby could have had two heads and she wouldn't have noticed; she could hardly bear to look. I struggled with her ambivalence. As the second and final child in a family of four I had never felt the utter desolation of being replaced; I regret now my lack of understanding. I would catch Wynnie staring at me and Caoimhe, longing perhaps for that perfect love that she imagined had been me and her, mother and child, before this troll, this creature, came along. Caoimhe's arrival was the limit of what she could bear. The guilt I felt at Caoimhe's diagnosis only muddied the foundations; not only had this new baby elbowed Wynnie sideways, but she was disabled to boot. I had saddled her with a slow and cumbersome dribbling thing, a sister to be ashamed of, for whom she must spend the rest of her life explaining, apologising. Any fantasies I'd had about three little girls playing happily, like extras from a Beatrix Potter screenplay, were crushed. I wanted to apologise for Caoimhe's existence, to fall prostrate at my daughters' feet and beg for their forgiveness, but of course I could not, and I felt impotent. There was nothing I could do; I had changed the course of their lives, had rewritten their history. I had given them a burden of care that would last the rest of their lives, a clause, a condition that would underwrite all the actions they took. These outdated beliefs, this panic, sprang from a speck of childhood memory that blew into consciousness: a buried sense of collective pity bestowed on a local woman and her child, held hostage by the needs of her other son, who had Down syndrome. These fears were soothed by an inner knowledge, an oak-hard surety that my experience was different; that Wynnie and Ellie would gain much more than they suffered. I knew this, because I knew them.

I am transported back to a Christmas past, the one before Caoimhe was born, when Ellie had asked for a particular type of handmade cloth doll that was popular at her Waldorf-based school. I wanted her to have one of those dolls, simple in structure, soft, warm, unique in appearance—the antithesis to the ugly plastic clones that wee and soil and burp on cue and line the aisles of toy superstores like some futuristic New Order. And so I made furtive trips at night to various doll-makers around Melbourne, but none I saw were of the right calibre for Ellie. The hemline, the eye line, the hair colour were not quite right. Conor sighed, just a little, at my crazy over-zealousness—bordering, some might say, on obsessiveness—in trying to find exactly the right doll. At last I found a woman who said she could make a doll to match my requirements, and two days before Christmas she presented me with the finished object. My stomach rotated under the impact of disappointment. She was ugly. Her hair was the wrong colour and the angle of her eyes made her look shifty. I couldn't change it. Christmas was hurling itself upon us like a loud scream and all I could do now was close my eyes and look away.

Ellie didn't love the doll immediately, but neither was she flung across the room in a Veruca Salt fit of pique. I saw the disappointment in her face on Christmas Day, and I marvelled at the quiet and thoughtful way she handled those feelings. I wondered if she knew it would have been okay to erupt, that the love between us was strong enough to override disappointment. She called the doll Molly. Theirs was a quiet love that grew, slowly, cautiously, built on the slow dawning that love has changing boundaries that can shrink or swell, capture or evict. I don't know what made Ellie finally love Molly, what mechanism one day set love ticking, but it didn't take too long before the doll acquired the frayed look of devotion, the grimed face of belonging. Two years later Ellie casually mentioned that she didn't like Molly's embroidered eyes, but this, I realised, had not stopped her loving her. I was in a dilemma. Should I change them or leave them? I changed them. There were shadows where the old eyes had been, giving Molly what cosmetic surgeons euphemistically call the 'tired look'. To be honest, the exposed material and pockmarked fabric where embroidery thread had been removed made Molly look like a teenage junkie. But Ellie was thrilled. 'She looks sleepy,' she proclaimed, putting her to bed, wrapped lovingly in her favourite green velvet skirt.

———

When Caoimhe was born, Ellie looked at her and said nothing. Months later I asked her what her first thoughts had been when she saw her sister at the hospital. 'She looked like an alien,' she said. 'Something about her eyes was funny. And she kept sticking her tongue out at me, which I thought was very rude.'

Ellie is a child who is conscious of difference. When she was two she started to complain of tummy aches, and a year later a biopsy revealed the villi in her gut were lying flat as a worn carpet. Her diagnosis of coeliac disease, a condition which required a radical change to her diet, has impacted considerably on her social life over the years. Ellie has grown up on parties where she has had to sit quietly, pretending not to care, while the rest of the guests eat cake, biscuits, buns and crisps that she is not allowed to touch. This has, I suspect, made her acutely sensitive to difference in a way that I have not experienced. At times I have a tendency to blunder around difference, loud and crass as a drunkard in my embarrassment, but she observes thoughtfully, quietly, sensitively. After parties, she developed a habit of going out on her scooter and, through the window, I would see her zooming up and down the drive, her mouth open and closing silently, hair streaming in the wind. This self-talk was her way of making sense of things, of filling in the gaps that I couldn't.

———

Sometimes I watch them together: Ellie—dark, beautiful and clever—with her sister, her opposite pole; unified, conjoined by what it means to stand out in a normal society. Ellie dresses Caoimhe up; she is, in the space of one afternoon, a fairy, a princess, a dog, a baby. I'm not sure Caoimhe understands the game, but she is happy to be with her sister, happy to be her dog. But my old pal, worry, pokes sticky holes in this tableau. Ellie has a rich internal world which she can enter in a trice: strange lands and places that whirr around her head with a giddy velocity, where scraps and fragments of the real world are scattered and rearranged at her bidding. Occasionally people may visit: her sisters and the next-door neighbours' children—ambassadors from their own foreign lands. But best of all is when they leave and she no longer has to mind her manners, give and take, share the dress-ups, the dreams. She is alone and needs no one in her independent state. A child's rich and vibrant inner world is, I like to think, a prophylactic against depression, a healing place for adult sickness, and so I nurture it. My worry is that Caoimhe will never be able to enter her own world, like Ellie, and can only ever be the bumbling accomplice in someone else's. The map to her own inner land is confusing and hard to follow; even if she finds the gateway, she must stand in muddy shoes on the periphery, unsure of what to do. Queen of the vast plain before her, but imprisoned by her handicap, like the ruler of a despot state under constant house arrest.

Still, I am heartened by watching her play with her sisters: their loving and fighting; their crude attempts at democracy exploding in brute force; their quiet moments slopping love around with a tender clumsiness. When Ellie was born I discovered a new kind of love, very different from the passionate yet essentially polite love that Conor and I enjoyed in courtship. It hit like a tidal wave hours after her birth: a wild, untamed, uncivilised love which threatened to drown me; for the first time I understood the terror of real power that comes in dealing with someone so utterly powerless.

And so I blundered through the foreign landscape of Ellie's early years, loving in this bewildering, primordial way. Out of rhythm, out of time, I struggled until the fear began to recede and I washed up on the shores of a new normality. I emerged from her babyhood shaken but strengthened by what felt like a near-death experience. The crisis of her birth revealed parts of me I had no idea existed: a protective instinct forceful as a magnet; a rage, a fury, as shocking as discovering oneself shopping in the nude; a frightening ability to hate as well as love. Ironically, her small and wrinkled presence girded my backbone in a way nothing else had over the years; her help-less being nailed me firmly to the earth, moulded me to its shape. The storm that was summoned with her arrival flushed out all the hidden crevices, and slowly, the flotsam and jetsam is receding in its wake. Seeing Ellie with Caoimhe reassured me that she, too, had survived the ravages of her babyhood relatively intact; she tends to her younger sister like someone who bears love's silver hallmark. For that I am glad.

It was easier with Ellie. She had been displaced once before; had burnt her tongue on the hot fury of realisation that mother-love, unlike marriage, is not exclusive. Also she was older, with a well-established circle of friends and her own backbone of resilience. She was able to explain Down syn-drome and her knowledge gave her status. And because none of her friends were too familiar with the condition, there was no one to go 'ughh!'

Amongst Ellie's circle, Caoimhe was loved and accepted, fought over and included. She was a model baby for a seven-year-old: easygoing, adorable, obliging and patient. She could be dressed up and lugged around the house, alert and smiley but not troublesome. In Ellie's eyes, she was the perfect play accessory.

With Wynnie, love grew slowly, erratically, but it did, eventually, grow. One day Wynnie asked me to bring Caoimhe to pre-school; she was dying to show off her little sister. Caoimhe sat in her capsule like a little alien and children gathered around. 'She's got funny eyes,' said a boy, looking at her. 'Yeah, your sister looks funny,' said another. The remarks were made without acrimony; they were just the natural observations of children who have not yet mastered the translation between thought and speech. Still, my insides shrivelled; I was hurting not for my child with the funny eyes, but for the one who was so proud of her, whose love had been hard won. I don't know if Wynnie heard the remarks; she was looking away.

The open wounds of the first few weeks scabbed over and a new skin grew underneath, delicate and thin. Among the five of us, Down syndrome ceased to be a trauma that divided us, and, for the most part, was just another piece in our everyday mosaic. But my testimony is not everyone's, and is subject to change. What is cute behaviour in Caoimhe now, what causes her sisters to stroke her hair and laugh, will probably embarrass them hideously as teenagers. How they chortle when she lovingly gives her bogies to their friends. How they will cringe when she does it to their boyfriends.

I have heard of adolescents who are at pains not to be seen with their disabled sibling, who swerve between shame and guilt. In times of panic I turn to research, which can be comfortingly unemotional. There are plenty of recent studies which paint a fairly positive long-term picture for brothers and sisters of children with Down's. One American study, admittedly only of sixteen sets of parents of children with Down syndrome, concluded that

> all parents reported that the experience of raising a child with Down syndrome had a profound impact on their life. More importantly, they reported that the positive consequences associated with this experience far outweighed the negative ones. Positive consequences included bringing the family closer together, learning the true meaning of unconditional love, putting things in proper perspective and appreciating diversity.

Interestingly, the report doesn't list the negative consequences. Thankfully, the last few decades have witnessed a paradigm shift; where earlier surveys darkly warned of siblings, especially older sisters, being damaged by the burden of care placed on them, and suffering from lack of parental care and attention, newer studies almost seem to recommend disability as a way of producing well-adjusted, empathic siblings—a sort of every-home-should-have-one attitude. I love the study which shows parental depression scores were lower in families of children with Down syndrome, and family functioning scores actually better:

> The results indicate that for many siblings, the experience of living in a family that includes a child with Down syndrome may be a positive, growth-producing experience. As a group, siblings in this study had above average self-concepts. In addition, maternal reports typically indicated that these siblings were socially competent, with a low incidence of behaviour problems.

I am not sure what 'above average self-concepts' means, but it sounds like something I'd want my girls to have, up there with healthy hair and nice skin. Another study, conducted in Manchester, England, showed 80 per cent of siblings of children with Down's had a positive relationship with their parents and their brother or sister. It is interesting that earlier studies painted a bleaker picture than those of today; it seems our level of compassion has increased in inverse proportion to our awareness of love's limits—while attempts to rid the world of Down syndrome plough onwards, there is an equal and opposite force being applied to improving life for those with the condition.

Perversely, what worries me most about our family dynamic is how much I will worry: now, and in the future. In this respect, research is no comfort: apparently, maternal stress is higher among mothers of children with Down syndrome, as are guilt levels. I am not sure I have room for more guilt and stress in my life; I am searching my pockets looking where to put it.

Of course reading reports is like listening to the wind in the trees; they tend to sway towards your own state of mind. Sometimes you have to look very hard to find your own, independent voice and make room for it to be heard. In the aftermath of Caoimhe's diagnosis, I dreaded informing relatives and especially the grandparents of her disability, and my gauche handling of it will not be found in textbooks or recommended in the research. I sent my mother an e-mail, seventeen days after Caoimhe was born, in which I off-handedly mentioned her condition, almost like a defiant postscript. Conor told his own parents one or two days after her birth. I am not sure how he did it; if they cried, or he cried. I believe there was some talk about angels from God. I read somewhere that it is best to wait, to allow the shock to settle among the crevices of your own flesh before passing it on to others, but I'm not sure how that works, when everyone's waiting with bated breath to hear that all is okay. I also read that one is supposed to empathise with the grand-parents' grief and disappointment, as they are not only mourning the loss of their own 'perfect' grandchild, but also hurting for their son or daughter too. I don't think this ever crossed my mind. The pain belonged to me alone and I self-ishly refused to share it. I preferred the relatives who just offered their congratulations and commiserations but steered clear, at least initially, of any gushing expressions of sorrow. Other people's tears were inappropriate and I felt an absurd obligation to comfort them.

When Caoimhe was six months old, Conor's parents came to visit us in Australia for Christmas. This was their first meeting with their newest granddaughter and I worried about their reaction to seeing her in the flesh: would they be stiff and awkward, dismissive even? Conor's father was a former deputy school principal, and academic prowess, I felt, was, in his eyes, one of the greatest achievements a child could have. I wondered how he'd view Caoimhe, future supermarket shelf-stacker. I feared she would glow dimly beside the other six glittering grandchildren, a flickering half-light, a half-person. I need not have feared; she was accepted and fussed over as much as her sisters had been. She was walked, rocked, sung to, smiled at and loved amid the heat and flies that plagued us that summer. During their visit I got food poisoning from eating roast turkey in 40-degree heat, sharing my plate with a variety of blowflies. Ellie was rude to her grandfather and mortified us all. Conor and his dad at one point got locked in a Mexican stand-off. It was all boringly, delightfully normal; mundane events were overridden by the shine of acceptance and the relief which can still lift me a notch higher when I think back to that time.

Caoimhe was two when we moved to Ireland, and my family came over from England and met her for the first time. My brother, a single, childless 40-year-old and delightful pianist, held her nervously, tentatively, as if he had been handed a small ticking bomb. Once he discovered her love of music he was happy to play the same nursery rhymes over and over again. He relaxed. They had found a common voice. My mother worked very hard, almost comically so, to be seen to be treating Caoimhe as 'normal'. Like Basil Fawlty in that immortal scene in *Fawlty Towers* when the German couple comes to stay and he's leaping around hissing at everyone, 'Don't mention the war!', so Caoimhe's disability became un-mentionable. Whatever she did, whether it was catching chickenpox, shouting 'No!' loudly in public places, or zig-zagging from room to room like a drunken bee, it was qualified immediately by my mother with 'But that's normal'.

There was the strange, and slightly perturbing, case of the Person Who Shall Remain Anonymous, who kept sending Caoimhe presents that were damaged, or somehow wrong: a shopsoiled hat, a jigsaw with pieces missing, mismatched clothes three sizes too big—perhaps a covert expression of anger at her perceived defects. Presents for my other daughters are always perfect. Other than that, aunts, uncles, cousins have bestowed on her only love and acceptance and pleasure at her being. This abundance of goodwill is money in the bank for Wynnie and Ellie; a silent assurance that their love for

Caoimhe is not misplaced or odd. I hope that unlike previous generations, they make it to adulthood unblemished by the scourge of pity, surely a death blow to sibling bonding. I am fortunate to have had such good experiences. I do not think other people are always that lucky. Not for a minute have I ever felt that Caoimhe's place in our extended family has been in doubt. Instead I believe she is truly loved and valued for what she brings: joy, fun, laughter, a restoration of harmony, a balance. Mental slowness is not the sum of her existence and how grateful I am that I am not the only one to recognise that.

Chapter 8
A Jumble of Ethics

I am reclining on a paper towel with something cold and hard between my legs. It is burrowing upwards and any second now my baby is going to appear as a smudge, a mole, on the blank face of the monitor positioned a few feet from my head. As the ultrasound transducer nudges onwards, the screen above crackles into life and there she is in her sac, like a tiny fried egg, hardly bigger than a punctuation mark, and my eyes film with tears.

It is a bizarre juxtaposition: she is both inside and outside, above and below me; six weeks into life and already omnipotent. I am hooked. It gives me a guilty thrill to invade her galaxy, her private domain, like unwrapping a secret, but my risk of ectopic pregnancy is high and I need to find out if she has become trapped somewhere in my damaged tubing. But she has made the road trip and landed in the womb.

But there is no decipherable heartbeat. So a week later I have another scan, this time performed by a dark-haired sonographer, the mother of two boys. We make empty chat, confetti words smoothing the passage of the damned transducer, a guided missile, seeking out my child. Once more the screen above begins to crackle. She is still there, a watchful eye blinking down at me. The blood has gone; reabsorbed by my body. But the heartbeat is very slow and not compatible with life. Conversation dries up.

We go home and I prepare for the death of a shooting star, a flickering match-head that traversed my body and exploded before I had time to grasp she was really there. Every five minutes I sneak off to check for blood. We have a birthday party for Wynnie, and I mechanically do the hokey-pokey. Afterwards I rush to the toilet to see if I am miscarrying. Back to the party to cut the cake; Happy birthday to you, squashed tomatoes and stew. Back to the toilet to see if I'm miscarrying. I am veering north and south like a crazy compass; celebrating the life of one child while waiting for the death of another. I go to the library and read about miscarriages; I want to know exactly how much blood I will lose, how much pain I can expect. I phone my friends who have had miscarriages. I am terrified. A nagging pain follows me round like a whining child; even at night I get no peace. I shift uncomfortably around in bed, convinced the baby is trying to drill its way out. My GP gives me her mobile phone number. We are all waiting for my body to break open and expurgate itself. I am snappy with tension. I write the baby a letter. I replay the memory of the scan, crystallising her insignificant presence in my mind: a fleeting glimpse of a life lost. The days drag; a turbulent, protracted wait. Elderly relatives remind me that in their day there was no prenatal testing, no way of knowing, as if their ignorance was their gain. All I know is that I am in a state of suspended grief: my life cannot move on until hers is over.

And then on one of those hot November days, when the heat blasts into every crevice, we are given the thumbs-up after yet another scan. The obstetrician, cool and crisp in a dazzling white shirt, shakes our hands and congratulates us, pleasure and awkwardness fuse in our grasp. The moment has all the formality of an award ceremony and I feel the need to flee. We escape the city and go and sit on the beach close to the water's edge where the sand is as heavy and wet as cement, pushing our bare toes into the gritty slush. I scrunch my eyes and stare at the faint thin line where sea meets sky; our future, her future, bright and vast and empty as the horizon.

At around eleven weeks we are offered something called maternal serum screening, to look for proteins and hormones with fancy acronyms freewheeling in my bloodstream. This, combined with an ultrasound to measure the amount of fluid at the baby's neck, will tell us our chances of having a child with Down syndrome. If it is high, I can have chorionic villus sampling: bits of the placenta are removed with a needle and examined under a microscope.

Or we can wait until I am fifteen weeks pregnant and have amniocentesis, a definitive, intrusive test which carries a 1 per cent risk of miscarriage. More instruments, more medics, more cold jelly on exposed belly. My head buzzes with facts and figures, plasticine numbers, which bend and stretch and shape to fit the pictures in my head. At 35, I have a 1 in 355 chance of having a child with Down's. This is significantly lower than the risk of losing my baby through intrusive testing, which is around one in two hundred. I imagine 355 women standing in a room and a giant hand plucking one from the masses. It wouldn't be me, couldn't be me! Ellie has coeliac disease (a 1 in 100 chance). Immediately after her birth, I developed thyroid disease (roughly a 1 in 1000 chance). I have already been plucked: sentenced to a lifetime of baking rice-flour muffins and the daily swallowing of little white tablets, but even though I irrationally believe it won't happen to me, I try to imagine what it would be like if it did.

Looking back, I guess I felt that raising a child with Down syndrome was something I could cope with. Surprisingly, it wasn't something Conor and I discussed. I think we knew one another well enough to know we'd get by. I had gathered enough scraps from Conor's life over nine years to understand that when it came to children, at least, we vibrated on the same note; we were both flawed but dedicated parents. Our relationship is not an easy one, we have fallen in love, fallen apart, taken an axe to our union and then sat down and rebuilt it, patiently, piece by piece. I knew all the patched up holes; the perilously worn bits in need of attention. I was proud of what we had constructed from the splinters. We had gone through the prospect of infertility to unexpected parenthood; we had emigrated; built a new life on a blank landscape; had alternated between financial hardship and relative affluence. Our relationship had been through many births and near-deaths, and stood, I now felt, battle-scarred, yet strong. We had learned to accept its imperfections. If a baby was born with a problem Conor would rise to the challenge; we both would. It didn't have to be talked about, neither was it just assumed; it was felt, resolutely, in every cell of my being.

Anyway, it wasn't going to happen to us!

I have to admit to having a discomfort about intellectual disability with roots tangled in childhood. I grew up in Cheshire in the north of England, close to an institution for the 'mentally handicapped', as it was known then. The home was an eerie place of peeling white buildings clustered around a chain-smoking chimney. It was a couple of miles from the nearest village, in the middle of nowhere, and when I cycled past it I always went a bit faster. Sometimes there would be a patient who stood at the entrance and shouted at the passers-by; he had mad hair that stood on end, like Kramer's in *Seinfeld*, and he always wore the same red-checked shirt.

The home used to hold summer fetes where you could go along and team up with a resident for the afternoon, which I did. Once. With much reluctance, when I was a teenager. Under pressure from my parents, who thought it would be good for me. The resident I was paired with was called Grace. She was sharp-featured and bird-like and she darted around and pecked at her clothes like a starling. She didn't have Down syndrome, but she had a tiresome obsession with ice cream. I queued for twenty minutes to buy her one from a motorised van and she promptly threw it on the grass. I bought her another and the same thing happened. I spent the rest of the afternoon steering her away from people with ice creams, because she would shout and try to grab them. This experience did not teach me compassion; it only heightened my sense of fear and made me tighten my grip on normality.

———

Over time, experience sanded away some of fear's sharp edges. Motherhood too, somehow softened and shaped me; the experience of being so loved taught me to be more magnanimous. A little boy in Ellie's kindergarten had Down syndrome; he was the first child with the condition with whom I had any contact, and perhaps it was my brief acquaintance with him that made me think it would be okay for me. I remember watching him on stage at the pre-school Christmas play; he was wearing spectacles and a Santa hat, singing 'Kookaburra Sits in the Old Gum Tree'—a lifetime away from my memories of Grace—and from the corner of my eye I saw his mother's tears sparkle on her cheeks and I felt my own tears well up behind a cemented smile. Perhaps I absorbed something from that scene: something I could not fully comprehend at the time, but filed away as important.

In the end, it was my understanding of where it was all heading that made me leap from the prenatal testing bandwagon. Leaflets the obstetrician gave me describing the various tests—the blood samples, the ultrasounds—made me feel I would be setting foot on a path fraught with anxiety, ultimately leading to the abortion of a malformed foetus, or the possible miscarriage of a healthy one. After much thought, I decided I couldn't go there, no matter what. Conor agreed. This was a subject we did discuss; as far as he saw it, amniocentesis was the only test that would tell us if the baby were healthy and the procedure carried too much risk. Neither of us would terminate, so what was the point? Besides, after all that we had been through, we couldn't face losing our baby again.

———

I am not a religious person, am not dictated to by a paternal God who has no role in raising my child. I have no time for right-to-lifers with their sensationalist placards, crappy slogans and accompanying baggage of displaced hurt and anger. Yet while I recognise the importance of legal abortion, there is something about terminating a child with a condition that is compatible with life I find difficult. For me, ending the life of a foetus with Down syndrome is ethically different from abortion in general; I see it as eugenics disguised as choice, where, in an impossibly short space of time, women find themselves in the role of society's bouncers, deciding who to let in or evict.

As a journalist I once wrote a feature about women who undergo late abortions. Part of my research involved attending a funeral service in a hospital basement for five foetuses that had been terminated due to chromosome abnormality. I remember the five tiny white coffins, like boxes of wedding shoes, laid out each with a rose on top; the tears of the mothers; the bowed heads of the fathers. I remember a hearse driving the coffins away to a plot in the middle of a sprawling graveyard, gaudily decorated with teddies and coloured plastic windmills spinning in the breeze; props of a childhood they were denied.

The ceremony in the basement was intensely moving, but nobody came to the cemetery. I followed the hearse to the graveside; my presence jarringly out of place; no parents to witness their disappearance into the earth, just an undertaker and a journalist in a Mitsubishi Nimbus, with a notebook in her bag. As I watched the coffins being lowered, a vaguely uncomfortable feeling crept over me, one I couldn't place, which tainted my sadness and choked my empathy. Today I recognise it as anger. Anger which felt misplaced; guilt-tinged, not allowed. Only minutes earlier I had witnessed for myself the parents' pain; the raw, genuine grief. Their tears, I see now, were not just for their babies, but for their own lost dreams; for themselves.

Down syndrome is never part of the parental fantasy, or at least it wasn't part of mine. I don't remember many of the fantasies I had about Caoimhe, other than her having red hair and playing the piano. Perhaps it was easier to see her as an individual because she was my third daughter, far more removed from me than the other two. I wonder how I would have felt if Caoimhe had been my first child, my only daughter, with the burden of my hopes and dreams and aspirations weighted on her shoulders.

Perhaps my chequered reproductive history has also played its part in improving my attitude towards disability; I still remember the brusque, white-coated obstetrician with the thick Dublin accent telling me, years ago, when children never featured in my life plan, that I would not have them naturally. After that, I never took pregnancy for granted.

———

Experience has shown me complexity where once I saw simple solutions. I have moved on from the Grace incident, have accepted that the rich tapestry of humanity needs variety; that while I hoped for a perfect child, it was not my entitlement; and that to remove people with Down syndrome from the landscape is like picking out the colour yellow.

What's left is the dark side of Down syndrome; the bit that gets tucked away in basements, shielded from public view. It's a stark reality; in Australia, 95 per cent and in the UK, 92 per cent of foetuses diagnosed with the condition are terminated and end up anonymous, discarded, in communal graves.

I have made many attempts to empty my feelings onto the page but all too often have hit the wrong note. There is something I want to say, to shout, but feel I cannot, gagged by the politics of a situation which is trigger-hot. In previous drafts I have skirted shyly around the issue; like a child in playground; dropping hints that go unnoticed; other times I have erupted; spitting venomous words onto the page which land like random drops of scalding lava. 'But what are you so angry about?' asks a friend.

Murder. The word seems absurdly incongruous with fleshy, life-giving pregnant women. Immediately I feel hated for saying it; the arguments are already beginning to rain down like rubble; snatches of phrase ricochet off my head— informed choice, difficult decision, heartbreaking—and my arms go up to shield myself.

You made your choice, the accusers cry. Let us make ours. I raise my hands in a gesture of peace. Okay, okay! But let me ask: were you really given a chance to make an informed choice?

I can't say I was, or at least only technically so. My pregnancy with Caoimhe, medically speaking, was a sophisticated process, compared with the other two; at my check-ups I was given glossy brochures in pastel shades describing the rudiments of high-tech tests and procedures; the importance of full bladders and getting someone to drive you home. Lunchtimes were spent on the Internet gorging on medical knowledge. Intellectually I was prepared to the hilt, but I don't remember reading much on the emotional aspects, the unfathomable dichotomy of loving your growing baby, while at the same time contemplating its death. This was a far cry from my pregnancy with Ellie: there was no Internet then, and, as were living in Ireland, where abortion remains illegal, no early detection of abnormalities.

At various stages in pregnancy my body has been objectified, invaded, scrutinised, monitored. I'll never forget, when I was expecting Ellie, the obstetrician slashing my belly with a huge black felt-tip cross. 'Get your husband to put his ear here and he can listen to the heartbeat!' I was branded. The faded imprint of the mark lingered for days.

Her first scan, over a decade ago now, was a grainy, weather storm affair, which I carried around, tattered and dog-eared in my purse. I showed it to anyone who would look, as if she wasn't in the privacy of my womb, but kept in a box, or a cupboard. You had to stare at the photo for a while before deciphering the image, like unscrambling a 'guess who' photomontage. Conor and I had strained our eyes at the fuzzy grey static vibrating on the screen; expectant, excited, like 1960s TV viewers watching the moon landing. With Wynnie, we were given giant negatives, black and shiny like x-rays, too big to keep in a purse. With Caoimhe, I discovered that scans have been taken to a new dimension. Now anticipated and routine, they are high-gloss, state-of-the-art affairs: a virtual model of the concealed baby is constructed on screen with a series of mouse clicks. I chose to have a scan at 19 weeks because there were questions I wanted answered: what was the sex of the baby, how well was it developing, how healthy was the baby's heart after its perilous start? I remember my anxiety in the days leading up to it, like an itch buried deep in my head, unreachable and slightly troublesome.

In a darkened room, I stare at my baby, oscillating like a happy seal, while the obstetrician roams her body, plotting graphs and measuring, zooming in and out like a quantity surveyor scouring the map of a building site. For a while anxiety smothers my love; I, too, find myself scrutinising the planes of her being with a foreign detachment. She is fine, we are assured. Growing normally. Perfect size for dates. As a finale, the obstetrician enthusiastically makes a 3-D model of her head for us on screen. It floats eerily in a black void, un-attached to a body. He rotates it slowly, with his mouse, talking animatedly about the wonders of such advanced technology. I stare at the slowly revolving head with damp enthusiasm. She looks ugly, like a papier-mâché skull

I once made with a balloon. And the hypothetical skin he has digitally designed for her is an odd brown colour, like paper soaked in tea. The face turns away from us and I smother a gasp. There is nothing at the back. She is a mask.

Ultrasound, I think, has a strangely divided role in both uniting and splitting a mother from her baby. I didn't have a 'nuchal fold' scan at eleven weeks, as many women do, but I have thought what it must be like: the foetus, bird-like but fully formed; squirming and turning; the parents cooing and gasping and doing all those new-parent things that used to be reserved for birth.

But unfortunately this test, along with a blood test, reveals certain 'markers'. A thickness at the back of the baby's neck, along with substances in the mother's blood, mean the preg-nancy is 'high risk'. More scans; and amniocentesis may be carried out. The mother can watch the screen as a giant needle punctures the baby's sac to extract fluid, its presence ugly and threatening—as a used syringe on a pristine beach. The baby stretches and turns, blithely unaware its days could be numbered. The scan's emphasis has shifted; it is no longer a 'bonding' experience. The mother must somehow split her-self off from the image of her baby in front of her, if she is planning to terminate. How else can she survive this experience? She is sent home and endures an agonising wait, her baby is no longer just a baby, but both baby and monster in turn. Meanwhile its chromosomes are stuck under a slide in a laboratory and counted: it is found to have an extra copy of chromosome twenty-one. The phone call comes; there is an awkward tension; I'm sorry, but the foetus has Down syndrome; now what would you like to do?

As I have said, in Australia, 95 per cent of foetuses found to have Down syndrome are aborted. In Victoria, where Caoimhe was born, the statistic is even higher: less than 2 per cent of women given the diagnosis continue the pregnancy. The baby that was wanted is no longer wanted; it has become a changeling, an impostor, a stealer of dreams. It can either be extracted, in parts, while the mother is asleep, or labour can be induced, causing premature birth. It is supposed to be born dead, but it may be born alive and then left to die, like an abandoned project. In some instances, the foetus is injected with potassium chloride by the surgeon, to kill it. In order to help the healing process, the parents may hold it, name it, see it.

In a frighteningly short space of time, the baby that was summoned into being, that was wanted and loved, has vanished, cut from the body like a malignant thing.

In an article that moved me to tears, a woman described terminating her baby, a girl, at 23 weeks, after discovering she had Down syndrome. She had undergone a scan at 20 weeks to discover the sex of her child, quite unprepared for anything else. Her partner was away so she went alone.

The scan showed two spots on the heart, which can indicate Down syndrome. She was sent home and told to return in four days to see the consultant. On the next visit he recommended an amnio, which was performed minutes later. The experience, which she described as awful, was performed in the blink of an eye, without much time for thought. The results came via a phone call three days later. The baby had Down syndrome. The woman returned to the hospital straight away, where she met with a different consultant. He gave her a bleak prognosis: her daughter would never be able to look after herself, and would be a burden on the rest of the family.

She decided there and then to terminate.

Melbourne writer and academic Kirsten Deane wrote about her daughter, Sophie, being diagnosed with Down syndrome in utero in the *Herald Sun*'s *Sunday Magazine*: 'Days earlier we had been handed photos of "our baby". Now we were discussing "terminating the pregnancy". I remember someone saying time was marching on if we wanted to "do something about it". The speed with which Sophie had gone from being a baby to a problem was mind-boggling.'

Deane and her husband went ahead with the pregnancy. A photo in the paper showed Sophie, robust and blonde, with her parents and younger brother. She didn't look at all like a problem.

Both women felt under pressure to act quickly as a result of their scans. I wonder how you can make life and death decisions in such an impossibly short space of time. I remember there was a point in my pregnancy with Caoimhe, somewhere around the tenth week, when the ground no longer felt firm beneath my feet; when the idea of having a baby with problems suddenly seemed overwhelming: 'I'm going to have a scan,' I told Conor that night. The next day the axis had tilted again: 'No I'm not.' I could discover the arrangement of my baby's chromosomes, but prenatal testing can tell you very little about the child you expect to have. It could not tell me how I'd feel about my baby, disabled or non-disabled; it couldn't predict my ability to love. The saddest part of the first woman's story was when she finally delivered her aborted daughter, fell in love with her instantly and didn't want to let her go.

I wonder if she would have gone ahead with the pregnancy if she had not been given such a bleak prognosis by the consultant. If someone had reminded her that unlike other chromosome disorders, Down syndrome is a condition compatible with life.

Like her, I was not inspired by the health professionals to think positively about Caoimhe. There were vague references to her being 'like her sisters' but no one told me that she might be capable of living independently; that perhaps she would ride a horse, play sport, the piano, violin, or whatever instrument took her fancy; that she might be able to travel independently on local trains and buses and hold down a variety of jobs. People with Down syndrome paint, sculpt, act, dance, sing. One of the best known is the late Judith Scott, an American woman who was institutionalised as a child. Scott became a sculptor; today her works fetch up to US$10,000 and are shown in galleries around the world. Another American with the condition, Jason Kingsley, was delivered by an obstetrician who told his parents he would never read or write; he went on to co-author a book about living with Down syndrome called *Count Us In*, together with fellow writer Michael Levitz, who also has Down's. In the UK, actor Paula Sage won a Scottish BAFTA for her role in the film *Afterlife*. Australian actor Ruth Cropper, who starred in *House Gang* and appeared in *A Country Practice*, was nominated for the Young Australian of the Year awards in 1998. And yet, as I write, I am aware that I am highlighting exceptional cases. As in mainstream life, not all boys with ginger hair become Boris Becker.

Since having Caoimhe, I have become as sensitive as a tuning fork to the tone and language of books that talk of her condition. Despite the ready availability of guidelines for writers and journalists (such as those posted on the UK's Down's Syndrome Association website), the term 'Down syndrome people' regularly appears in the media.

I read a book on prenatal testing, first published in 2006, which begins its section on Down syndrome by reminding us that it was 'previously called mongolism'. I try to imagine a book which starts 'African Americans, previously called niggers . . .' The word Mongol—like the word nigger—was deleted from acceptable vocabulary several decades ago. It was banned from World Health Organization publications in 1965; I wonder what purpose this historical reminder serves in a book published forty years later and aimed at young women of a different generation?

The glossary of the same book describes Down syndrome as a condition which 'results in severe intellectual handicap and commonly other physical abnormalities'. I choke on my own outrage. Down syndrome can result in profound intellectual disability, but only in 10–15 per cent of cases. The vast majority of people have mild to moderate impairment and some have normal intelligence.

Anyone who doesn't have a child with a disability may consider that I am being umbrageous; like an oversensitive car alarm, I ring shrilly at the merest touch, the slightest knock, resulting in a collective groan from the neighbours. But I am one step ahead of my daughter; sweeping the litter from her path, the discrimination, the prejudices, because she doesn't need these additional obstacles which belong to a different era, a different headspace.

In an article in the UK's *Sunday Telegraph* on late-term abortions, a spokesperson from the Down's Syndrome Association complains that medical professionals have failed to keep pace with advances in prenatal testing: 'Some health professionals have outdated or prejudiced views about people with Down syndrome, owing to a lack of training about the condition,' said the spokesperson, 'so they are unable to provide a balanced view on what life would be like for the family of a child with the condition.'

After Caoimhe was born, I was asked, many times, if I had had testing in pregnancy. The questions from medical staff started in the hospital, only hours after her delivery. Over the days that followed, they gathered momentum; for a while they were persistent and depressing. Friends would ask; not close ones, who either knew, or were sensitive enough not to ask, but curious ones, acquaintances, who banked on the periphery. There was an assumption that prenatal testing had let me down, failed in its duty; the tone went up an octave when it was discovered I hadn't had any in the first place. Oh!

Disability, and particularly learning disability, is generally considered a bad thing; this must be so, otherwise prenatal testing wouldn't exist. In the UK, a screening service for abnormality is now offered to all pregnant women at an estimated cost of £15,300 for every detected pregnancy affected by Down syndrome. Despite this, the birth rate for affected babies remains static. One author with expertise in this area admits that cost benefit is an important factor in the introduction of tests. This, the author acknowledges, is like putting a price tag on various abnormalities, but it would be irresponsible not to do so; individuals with Down syndrome are living longer and need care long after their parents are able to provide it. He points out: 'Down syndrome babies are a major cost to the community and may cause a family considerable financial and emotional hardship.'

I ponder this statement. Do considerations of this sort do justice to human beings? Down syndrome has a lower cost per capita than most chronic disabilities. Rarely, I imagine, do people with the condition have drinking problems or smoking-related illnesses. They do not cause environmental damage by driving fuel-guzzling cars. They are unlikely to squander our tax funds languishing in jail. The author warns that people with Down syndrome are at a higher risk of Alzheimer's and leukaemia but does not point out that they are at a lower risk of contracting age-related cancers than the 'normal' population and will not require the expensive drugs that one in three of us will demand when we develop carcinomas in old age.

I can't help feeling that prenatal testing has become similar to childhood vaccination programmes, a sort of seek-and-destroy exercise that the medical profession has deemed necessary for general health. But in order for it to be truly effective—if we are to rid society of its scourge—we must all obediently follow suit.

In the *Sunday Telegraph* article, one mother-to-be talked of her shock at discovering her baby had Down syndrome while undergoing amniocentesis at 35 weeks—worse, she was 'appalled' by the doctor's response: 'He urged us to think about the termination and think about how having a baby with "mental retardation" would affect our lives. He listed only the potential negatives about Down's syndrome, without giving us any information to read for a more balanced view.' Two weeks later her son was born healthy.

I too feel reproved: I did not consider the effects on the wider community when making my decision not to have pre-natal testing, knowing that at my age I stood a higher chance of a problem pregnancy. On an English radio programme, a bioethicist from a university in the north of England tells us: 'Eugenics is the attempt to create fine healthy children and that's everyone's ambition.' He believes women who choose to have babies even when there are problems are 'misguided' and the more we can screen out pain and suffering, the better.

While I didn't know Caoimhe had Down syndrome, my decision not to have testing implied my willingness to give birth to a faulty child. I've really screwed up the system. I am the rebel in the back row who's disrupting the smooth order of the classroom by refusing to conform. I didn't have the tests and now I have a baby who is not 'fine'. One who is going to place a considerable burden on our smart, shiny society. Funding and skills will have to be leached from the pot and spent on my broken, unwanted offspring. I feel the reproach-ful eyes of the paternal hierarchy fall upon me: 'It's not funny, Evans. Your irresponsible actions have spoilt it for the whole of the class.'

Women today come under unbearable pressure to produce perfect babies; we are bombarded with images and information telling us how our children should look, should be. In an address to the Australian Press Club, Julian Savulescu, Professor of Practical Ethics at Oxford University, talked about how we should be using science and medical tech-nology, not just to prevent and treat disease, but to enhance people's lives. 'I want to suggest to you that we should make happier, better people.'

Even 'normal' is no longer good enough. Savulescu argues that parents of a child with a 'stunning intellect' who, through dietary neglect, cause it to have only a 'normal' intellect are guilty of parental abuse. 'But failing to institute some diet that would cause a normal child to have a stunning intellect results in exactly the same thing: a child who's normal, who could have been much brighter, I believe is equally wrong.'

I see myself in handcuffs being led away, guilty as charged. I don't give my children vitamins regularly, not even Caoimhe. I give them fruit and vegetables, but nowhere near enough. Over the years I have tried various 'health' supplements and wasted money on bottles of foul-tasting gunk that still lurk in the recesses of my fridge. We have had fights over taking these life-changing, money-draining elixirs. I have raised my voice and worn my 'vinegar face', as Ellie calls it. Afterwards I have been remorseful, knowing my vinegar face is now imprinted on their brains, associated with health. I have probably created an eating disorder or two.

My concern is that this current ideology, which says that even normal is no longer good enough, makes the termination of children with disabilities not only socially acceptable but generally encouraged. If this chapter has a bitter taste to it, it is because I have been forced to confront a reality that I'd rather not. My child is not wanted by the vast majority of people in the world she inhabits, is considered not good enough, is feared and loathed underneath a sickly sentimentality, and it hurts.

I wonder why Down syndrome is so despised among the bright stars, the upper echelons of intelligence. I suspect because it is the enemy of intellectualism. The cleverer the world becomes, the more we shun those who do not inhabit the same space, much in the same way whites once used apartheid to segregate black people because they thought them intellectually inferior.

The desire to stamp out Down syndrome can be traced back more than a hundred years. At the turn of the twentieth century, a Chicago physician, Dr Harry Haiselden, argued that difference was unnatural and its continuation was to be avoided. Haiselden refused to operate on babies he considered 'defective' and described children born with Down's, as well as those with hydrocephaly, microcephaly and spina bifida, as 'monstrous' and 'hideous'. Their continuation, he said, would be an affront to nature.

In 1981, Dr Leonard Arthur was prosecuted in a criminal court in England after he let John Pearson, a baby with Down syndrome, die days after his birth.

On discovering their baby's condition, the parents rejected him and Dr Arthur prescribed high doses of a painkilling drug to be administered at regular intervals. The baby's clinical notes read: 'Parents do not wish baby to survive, nursing care only.' At the doctor's trial, Sir Douglas Black, then president of the Royal College of Physicians, told the jury he thought it was ethical 'that a child suffering from Down syndrome should not survive'. Dr Arthur was acquitted amid much celebration.

The Australian ethicist Peter Singer, Professor of Bioethics at the University Centre for Human Values, Princeton University, has frequently spoken and written about his interest in infanticide over the years. While he does not automatically advocate it for babies with Down syndrome, in his book, *Rethinking Life and Death*, he argues that the prospects for a child with the condition are clouded right from the start:

We cannot expect a child with Down syndrome to play the guitar, to develop an appreciation of science fiction, to learn a foreign language, to chat with us about the latest Woody Allen movie, or to be a respectable athlete, basket-baller or tennis player.

After I read this my jaw dropped. Does understanding Woody Allen really improve life's prospects? Does actually being Woody Allen hold better life prospects? Divorced from his wife, accused of sexual abuse, married to his step-daughter, Allen's life has not escaped the same gamut of emotions as the rest of us simply because he is a comic genius.

————

There is plenty of evidence that even in this day and age, paradoxically, people with Down syndrome still suffer at the hands of the medical profession. In 1999, the British Down's Syndrome Association carried out a survey that found 28 per cent of parents were highly dissatisfied with medical pro-fessionals caring for their children. An independent inquiry published in April 2001 found that children with Down syndrome being treated for heart problems at two major UK hospitals were 'less favoured' because of their condition.

In an editorial in the British Medical Journal, Savulescu concedes:

It is probably unlawful to place a lower priority on children with Down's syndrome and other disabilities who need heart transplants, but is it unethical? . . . Whether disability such as Down's syndrome should be considered relevant in allocating a scarce resource turns on how much the disability associated with it detracts from a good life.

I have no idea how a medical team judges what makes a good life. I wonder if police checks are performed on transplant patients: 'I'm very sorry Mr Smith, but we see you have a record of GBH. Down you go to the bottom of the queue.' What about those who smoke? Where do they come on the list? How on earth does a doctor begin to make such an ethical judgement?

Savulescu acknowledges this difficulty, arguing 'a tolerant and affluent society would strive to provide quality of access to everyone for as many interventions as possible'.

Soon it may be a moot point. In Australia, work is being done to produce an earlier test for Down syndrome, performed at around five or six weeks, which would examine isolated foetal cells scraped from the cervix. This test will alleviate the risk and pain of late-term abortions. As three-quarters of pregnancies affected by Down syndrome spontaneously end in miscarriage, one wonders at the economic value of such an early test. And it spreads before us a new picnic of ethics. Could a simple test that frees us from the trauma of mid- or late-term surgical abortion herald the end of Down syndrome, a condition that's been around since human life began, or longer? Apparently, chimpanzees and gorillas give birth to offspring with trisomies; the extra chromosome was part of our genetic make-up even before we parted ways with our ape ancestors. Will children like Caoimhe soon be erased from the picture, rubbed off the page like a child's stick drawing, with little or no thought as to how to bring them back? I cannot bear to imagine a life without Caoimhe, I try and the thought slips off the edge of consciousness, like the yolk of a sunset disappearing into the sea.

One of the ways women deal with the guilt of termination is by telling themselves it is best for the baby. Some women feel their child would be subject to a lifetime of suffering and that aborting them is averting a bigger tragedy. On the net are entire websites dedicated to the outpourings of grief of people who have terminated their foetuses; Down syndrome often has a special category all to itself. The same theme is repeated again and again: parents are somehow saving their child from a life worse than death. One woman talks about holding her aborted baby, who was born alive, naming him Joseph, and admiring the familial genetic make-up of his nose before he died: 'I told him I loved him with all my heart and hoped he understood what I was doing was out of love for him.' Another woman wrote: 'Our baby would have had a tough and painful life ahead of him if we chose to continue the pregnancy.'

Would he? Who knows, in that particular case, but generally, the idea that children born with Down syndrome suffer a poor quality of life is as outdated these days as the term 'mongol', and yet it seems to have left an indelible imprint. The reality is that few children with Down syndrome suffer; it is the parents' self-esteem that suffers, in a world where perfection is increasingly important. 'Will £1000 get you an Alpha baby?' asks the headline in *Grazia* magazine. Underneath, midwife Zita West, founder of something called the 'Better Baby' programme, argues, 'Science shows you can create a better baby and that you can give him or her the best potential for life.'

What happens if the child fails to live up to such high parental expectation? I imagine the weight of responsibility on these alpha babes to succeed in life must be considerable—no jobs as shelf-stackers for them! This, however, is the 'best' Caoimhe can look forward to, if the experts are anything to go by. One doctor told me, quite bizarrely, that she might get work in a garden centre—she was just a few months old at the time.

Perhaps I am lulled into a false reality by my divine experience of Caoimhe; I must guard against sounding evangelical. Not long ago I was sitting in a café with Conor and the girls. Caoimhe's mouth was muddy with chocolate and Wynnie and Ellie were munching contemplatively on crisps. We had just been for a walk on a pale, damp autumn morning; wet leaves still clung to our boots as we warmed our hands around ceramic cups. Across the café was another family silently sitting: the mother's face was a powdered puffball that had begun to wizen, her hair glued into spiky shapes; her fat husband, in a brown anorak, sat opposite, damp and shapeless as a puddle. Tucked next to the table in a plastic capsule was a baby clad in many shades of blue—a boy then—but it was the teenage daughter, who had Down syndrome, who drew me in. She too was plump and shapeless, with a haircut that Ellie grew out of five years ago. She was eating a sausage roll, so slowly that I watched with fascination as she raised it to her lips; with all the energy of a leaking battery. Nobody talked. I immediately turned to Caoimhe: 'Do you like the chocolate, Caoimhe? Yummy chocolate! Some for mammy? What? No? Oh, just a little bit!' Ridiculous babble, irritating as bad radio. The family's silence triggered in me a verbal overload.

What if Caoimhe were like this girl; so slow and silent and

disengaged? She appeared completely cut off from her sur-
roundings, as if the effort of eating that sausage roll sucked
her from the rest of the world. Meanwhile Caoimhe, having
finished her chocolate, was circling the café, wheeling from
table to table like a grinning seagull, scavenging for scraps.

———

I thought about this girl for ages afterwards. Did her mother
wish she hadn't had her? She had showed the girl no attention, but likewise, she had hardly noticed the baby, surely her
grandson, either. If Caoimhe had been one of the 10–15 per
cent of babies with Down syndrome who were profoundly
affected, who reached her teenage years struggling to eat a
sausage roll, would I be writing a different book? Would I be
looking back wistfully on the choices I'd made in pregnancy,
wishing I had done it differently?

On the subject of termination, so emotionally charged, there
is no right or wrong, only sadness. I shout murder, but timidly,
apologetically, uncertainly, because I realise the jumble of ethics
is so tightly knotted it can never be unravelled by a single word.

Recently the mother of a 20-year-old girl with Down
syndrome wrote honestly about her experiences in the UK's
Sunday Times magazine: 'There are people who make
wonderful parents of Down's syndrome children, and there
are others who just find it too painful.'

She went on to catalogue her pain, which has remained
damp and raw: 'I've done my best, which is what you do as a
mother, but I grieve almost every day. That's not to say I don't
love her, but I mourn the child I'd hoped for.'

Like her, I have learned that being the mother of a child with a disability involves pain. Having Caoimhe has shattered my defences, exposed the dark and ugly bits of me, the bits that could have remained buried all my life, if she had not come along. This book is really nothing more than my attempt at rebuilding myself from the pieces she has cracked apart to expose the truth of who I am. Now here I stand: bigot, narcissist, control freak—and so begins the slow road to healing. I don't want to be grieving when she's twenty.

I am fortunate to be able to cope; to be able to look at my shadows, even blacker against the light of her being; to wince; to cringe; to get down on my knees and scrub. I can do this because I have trudged through years of therapy, which has wrenched truths from their hiding places and given me more of a capacity to deal with pain and grief. I am also lucky to have an emotionally switched-on partner with a vast reservoir of love. Not everyone is that lucky.

There is no escaping grief, whatever you do. Termination is only the beginning of a different kind of sorrow. In the article that moved me so much, it was sorrow rimed with guilt. The writer felt the experience of tragedy had turned her into a darker person: she didn't want the power of deciding the fate of another human being, and the consequences of her actions have tainted her with shadows that only she understands. The secret of her baby's short existence has left her marooned, stranded, stuck in a place where silence hangs over the unfinished discussion, because abortion remains taboo. To me, the consequences of her actions seem huge and profound; a lifetime's burden of a different sort.

While the pain of Caoimhe's diagnosis is something that will never leave me, at least I have the exquisite pleasure of her being, the joy of her life, to counteract it. I can talk about the pain, share it. It is not a lonely secret buried inside. I wonder what it would be like to be left wondering, not knowing; for a life to end on such a terrible note with no postscript, nothing to heal.

I guess there is no rational solution, no easy get-out clause for seemingly intractable personal problems muddled by love. For love makes no sense when analysed intellectually. It is shapeless and weightless as it slips through your fingers, unable to be appraised and costed and measured. The woman in the article discovered she could love her disabled child too late; no one had told her it was possible.

I am glad that I did not discover that my flame-haired, piano-playing fantasy daughter had Down syndrome during pregnancy. Right from the start, holding Caoimhe has been my strength, my normality.

She will never be a monster, is not hideous, or defective. Recently I got into the habit of calling her Ki-Ki. The other day she turned round to me and said firmly: 'No Mammy. Not Ki-Ki. Caoimhe.' She knows who she is. She has a voice and it is missing from the literature that bleakly and erroneously debates what it is to have Down syndrome. I don't ever remember being told that she would have a voice, or that her being could give me a voice. That living with her would reveal deeper, buried parts of myself I never knew were there.

Being told the problems that a child *in utero* may face once born is a world away from watching these challenges unfold on a daily basis, so slowly—like sea water chiselling rock, you hardly notice. I am beginning to be aware of the difficulties Caoimhe faces, the help she is going to need. She struggles with mobility, cannot run and play like her more robust friends; her neck gets sore, her nose is perpetually snuffly. There are, I suspect, more diagnoses ahead, possible operations to confront, therapies to endure. These things would have alarmed me when she was just a photograph, a mystery guest in the womb, but now they are experiences I feel I can face: our emotional history will propel us through.

My life is not too dissimilar to that of any other mother of a two-and-a-half-year-old. Once a week I take Caoimhe to a playgroup, where I have made friends with another mother who faces the same sort of battles and dilemmas as I do. We both suffer from bouts of occasional boredom and a frustration with running noses, wet days and piles of washing. She has her problems, I have mine; we both lead flawed lives. Here in County Down, on a typical Monday morning, we paint with our respective toddlers and spit out our particular gripes. There are times when we are gloomy as we drink tea, worn down by a Monty-Pythonesque move-your-coat-to-the-lower-peg style of bureaucracy that pervades sections of the Northern Irish health system. We punctuate our conversations with fragments and anecdotes snatched from our previous child-free lives and they lift us like brief splashes of pale spring sunshine. I love to brag of celebrities I once rubbed shoulders with, places I have been to; she, an astrophysicist in her previous life, talks about planets and galaxies and formulas that carry secrets, like Einstein's $E = mc^2$. Anything can be transformed, given the right environment. Life as we know it evolved because of a collision of intricate, timely events. The dust and rubble that litter the heavens, the molecules and atoms, spewed out from exploding supernovas, have combined and spun themselves into a ball we call Earth. We are all made from the grit of these ancient stars, all composed of the same basic elements. But, as the author C. S. Lewis once wrote, this is not what a star is, only what it is made of. For me there is something else, some essence that is timeless and mystical, that eludes my understanding no matter how much it is explained to me; as if all things are intertwined to make a cosmic whole, some manifestation of a basic oneness.

Sometimes, when I look at Caoimhe, I get it.

Chapter 9
The Holywood Ending

It is one of those insufferably hot Melbourne evenings, the kind that makes me feel bad-tempered and aggressive as I defend myself from the omnipresent heat. I have spent the best part of a day sweltering in my poky, un-air-conditioned study, traipsing the Internet, and have stumbled across a paper looking at the effect of Alzheimer's on the brains of adults with Down syndrome.

I have read many papers about Caoimhe's increased risk of Alzheimer's, but this one in particular seems to suggest it is a foregone conclusion, a sure thing, like wrinkles and unsightly veins for the rest of us. I download her fate onto the printer and make a cup of tea. Tea goes much better with bad news than with good. My heart rate triples as I read the pages; she may well live to over 50, but brain rot will set in way before that. She'll be too confused to know her name, so what's the point? Childhood is her honeymoon, before the dark clouds bank on the periphery of middle age. I slump forward on my arms; grief encases me like cement.

I am aware that the Internet is bandit country and I, like a naive tourist, have wandered off from the rest of the party and been well and truly lynched. I have no idea whether this paper I found by chance is reputable research or not; but what I do know is that insecurity makes me susceptible to bad news, so that possible scenarios become the inevitable last acts of the tragic dramas of my mind. Knowing this does not make me feel any better; neither does my trusty companion, my cup of tea. I am marooned in misery. I sit with my head in my hands for several minutes before my eye catches sight of my watch. It is three pm and I must slap on my 'cheerful mother' face and manoeuvre myself out to the kitchen to bake a batch of muffins. The girls are due home from school: hot, hungry and with quivering antennae that can pick up the merest subtlety of mood change. And so, for the next four hours or so, I stuff the research into a dark spot in my head and try to be a Nice Mother. I wonder how good I am at it; occasionally I catch a glimpse of myself in the mirror and am alarmed at my fixed manic grin and irregular, angled eyebrows. How could I fool anyone?

But now it is late; the girls have gone to bed and the dreaded research which I have tried so hard to contain is spilling over and trickling down my brain; a persistent *drip-drip*, corrosive as battery fluid, no longer dammed behind a grinning wall. I am fearful and the fear makes me angry— that and the damned weather. It's been in the high thirties for four days running and the bricks are as hot as a tandoori oven. And so here I sit at the end of the day, with another cup of tea and a candle, and Conor for company, trying to explain to him the awfulness that waits, like the big bad wolf, for Caoimhe to come skipping through the woods.

But he is not listening. I can barely get a grunt of acknowledgement out of him. He is not even looking at me; he sits at right-angles to me with his hands clasped and his eyes on the carpet in that frustrating way he has, as if he is bracing himself against the attack of my winged thoughts. I hate him when he is like this; he is the worst kind of audience—a blank face, a mystery within. In my head I am beating my fists against the shop window but it remains firmly shut. My thoughts no longer flutter in the air between us like doves; they bomb the glass like something from Hitchcock—but Conor remains impenetrable. The birds move in, more menacing, more desperate. There is a crack in the glass; Conor stirs and sighs and says something which implies that I shouldn't be wasting my time worrying about a disease that might happen in thirty years, by which time a cure would surely have been found anyway.

'Not might happen! Will!' I yell, forcefully, dramatically. Because this has been brewing, building, since three o'clock that afternoon. After the girls went to bed I lay in the bath long after the water drained away, working out the impossible conundrum of whether it is better for me to outlive Caoimhe, or her to outlive me; imagining the horror of us both with Alzheimer's, unable to recognise each other. By the time it gets to this point—nine o'clock on a January night and still no sign of a cool change—I am ready to break.

(Note to other couples: Conor and I have very different approaches to dealing with disturbing information. I ruminate on it, chew it, spit it out, chew it again and too often choke on it. He tends to distance himself from anything that goes off his radar, as if by doing so it won't happen. Neither is the best approach.)

'Don't you care?' I shout now. 'She's not even two!' he shouts back. And here we are, finally looking at each other, all jarring angles and pointy bits and I am aware, for a split second, how anger uglifies us: his hair sticks out at odd angles where he has clawed it in frustration, and his expression is the same wounded one that my mother used to wear when I offended her. Guilt from the past as well as the present combines to fuel the furnace of my anger; I am aware my brows are puckered and gathered unflatteringly and my hands are on my hips like some battleaxe schoolmarm. Conor and I are a unified beast made up of the demons of each other's fantasies.

In the middle of the shouting the phone rings. We let it go to the answering machine, each of us so locked in our fight we cannot move; there is nowhere to go outside of it. We hear the voice of Conor's dad beneath the decibels of our rage: it is a low, sad voice; we cannot make out the words but the tone summons us from our battle and the beast vanishes fast as a fairy tale.

We replay the message. It is bad news. Conor's father has cancer and the prognosis is bleak. Now we are clinging to each other and weeping. Caoimhe's future, which had loomed so threateningly close, has receded to where it belongs. This is the knife-edge present: awful, terrible and gleamingly pristine. I am standing starkers in a moment of reality, and the honesty of it makes me feel ashamed.

It was hard to sleep that night. Conor's parents, despite being geographically far away, have always been part of the close weave of our lives. They were there after Wynnie and Caoimhe were born, arriving at our house with suitcases, sun hats and strong arms to rock the babies while we ate and slept. There were regular Sunday phone calls, e-mails and updates, and enough easy banter and the sharing of lives to make the distance seem bearable. But now it wasn't.

Conor's parents suddenly seemed very far away; they may as well have been on Mars. The ending of a life is as sacred as a beginning, and the more we talked, the more we realised we wanted to be part of this crisis. Ever since we'd arrived in Australia ten years earlier with a rucksack, a foetus, and not much else, we had planned to return, someday. After Caoimhe's birth the question mark that hung over our future became more urgent, but still we had not made any concrete plans, partly because our finances were so precarious, but mainly, I think, because we were happy where we were. The question of living in Ireland hummed about on the periphery of our consciousness like an easy lodger, never really making excessive demands. Then came Caoimhe's birth and now the news of Conor's dad and we finally decided to act.

We would move to Ireland for a trial run of at least six months. In a spooky act of synchronicity, shortly after we made the decision we had a call from our landlord to say our house was to be pulled down and reincarnated as a shiny new block of apartments. This had been on the cards for years, but we had got used to living with the uncertainty. Like Ireland, the future of our house was a dubiety that hovered in the hinterland; there for another day. Now that day, too, was upon us. It felt as if our life in Australia was beginning to be rubbed out.

Career-wise, I had taken unpaid leave from my job as a feature writer with *The Age*, so that I could write this book. It was proving exceedingly difficult, but at least I could attempt it from any point on the globe. Conor was floundering through his PhD. But he, too, could flounder anywhere on the globe. It was, we felt, a good time to at last experiment with life in Ireland.

We broke it to the girls, selling it as an adventure, dressing it up in frills and whistles, painting it pink, because that was the dominant colour in our house. 'There will be horses,' I said to Ellie, coaxingly. Ellie loves horses but we couldn't afford riding lessons in Melbourne, and the nearest riding school was forty minutes away in any case. In my mind's eye I saw velvet green fields stuffed with fat ponies—dappled, bay, brown and piebald—and Ellie trailing through daisy-wet grass, clutching apples. I didn't see the mud and the perennial rainfall and months of unemployment which meant we had to scrabble for pennies to pay for the horse-riding. How could I, on a 38-degree day in inner-city Melbourne, when misty rainfall seemed overwhelmingly attractive, and joblessness, with our combined qualifications, an absurdity.

We had to work out where to settle. Conor's parents live in Dundalk, but we wanted the girls to continue in Steiner education to keep disruption to a minimum. There are only three Steiner schools in Ireland; the nearest one to Conor's family was in Holywood, a small town outside Belfast. So that is where we would live.

I raided the Internet for information. On the computer screen Holywood looked lovely: an ancient town bordered by bumpy green hills spread with gorse on one side and coast-line on the other. Apparently C. S. Lewis got his inspiration for Narnia by looking out across the crooked teeth of the Mourne Mountains from the top of the Holywood Hills. I was excited; Ellie and I had enjoyed *The Lion, the Witch and the Wardrobe*, and now I could tell her we were going to live in Narnia. She didn't seem as excited as I'd hoped. I told her again: 'Narnia! Imagine that!' She clearly couldn't. I may as well have told her we were going to live in the Wardrobe. Some places are best left to the imagination, because when you are nine years old they are not worth uprooting your home for.

Autumn blazed upon us. The girls and I gathered huge
gold and bronze leaves and made leaf rubbings to hang on the
wall, death masks of summer. We found gumnuts and glued
wooden beads on top to make fairies. And all the time I was
immersing myself in this molten vignette, I was uncomfortably poked by memories of autumns from my own youth:
damp, soggy affairs with clods of dull brown leaves shrouding
dog poo in the gutters. It was all ahead of us.

I continued to write, and when I didn't write I sorted
through ten years of junk, working out what to sell, what to
keep. We had amassed a huge pile of crazy stuff considering
we had arrived with nothing. It ran like a narrative of our life
in Australia with interludes and intermezzos thrown in from
our past: I noticed how bright we had become over the years,
muted clothing giving way to more tropical shades; even our
bedding, our crockery, had become quite jazzy. I loved the
colours of Australia: the deep, uninterrupted blue of the sky,
the fried egg and baked bean sunsets and the purple electric
storms. When I closed my eyes and thought of Ireland, I saw
leaky black.

One fine autumn day we laid out various fragments from
our life story on the front lawn and had a garage sale; I winced
when people came to stare, to leaf through our things with
expressions that ranged from disdain to curious interest. My
clothes, I noticed, aroused the most disdain; I think I sold one
thing, which made me wonder about my wardrobe all these
years. Perhaps I should have stuck to black. The girls' toys sold
in droves: the pair of old school desks I had never managed
to restore; the toy oven I bought for Ellie's second birthday;
the heaps of early learning stuff I had succumbed to in my
manic 'make every moment a learning opportunity' phase.

Ellie and Wynnie were excited by the garage sale. They collected feijoas from the tree at the bottom of the garden and sold them in brown paper bags. They watched the props of their childhood being carted off through the front gate; only in the aftermath were there tears for the casualties: Rebecca, a doll that Wynnie treasured, had been swept away by accident; a doll's house, a Christmas present, had been sold for ten dollars, a decision that Ellie still regrets.

Departure Day—June 8—rolled towards us like a bowling ball while we waited in a mix of fear and excitement. We invited removalists to come and give us their quotes: one posh chap surveyed our eclectic mix of St Vincent de Paul furniture with a snooty eye; I think his clients were more usually the local jet set. He had been fooled by our posh Brighton postcode into thinking we were something that we weren't. A man from a rival firm came with a ginger toupee, shiny suit and clipboard. He moved through the rooms with an appraising eye, ignoring the children's questions, spouting his sales patter in a dull monotone, oddly detached until he saw our cat, at which point he became quite animated, even friendly. He was a cat person. Had one himself. Fed it the best there was. Sheba, or something like that. Missed him when he went to work (the cat that is, not him).

Ah yes, the cat. Alfie had been Wynnie's third birthday present. We had got him from an animal shelter, hoping for a kitten; at the age of one he was the closest we could get. Alfie and I did not always have the best of relationships; I loved him until the day he jumped from the washing machine and broke his leg. I have heard of cats falling from great heights and landing on their feet; it seems Alfie couldn't leap three foot. The vet's bill came to $1000; I handed the money over;

my face clamped with the effort of doing so. I was pregnant at the time; this was the money I'd been saving for Caoimhe.

Alfie's broken leg saga paralleled my difficult pregnancy: the bone didn't knit properly, he had a pin inserted and physio. I would drop him off for his appointments, my own back aching with the weight of pregnancy.

Still he limped, a symbol of hurt pride, his wounded dignity. He hated my being pregnant, the way I would push him away because the smell of him made me nauseous; he was no longer allowed to sleep on our bed at night.

When Caoimhe was born he sniffed her cautiously, then ran away and hid. A few days later, I noticed a stench, sharp and acrid. Then I smelt it again, in a different room. Cat's urine has an unbelievable odour and soon the whole house stank. We took him back to the vet, a young man with a pony-tailed fiancée, a smart car, but no tact, only to be told, rather severely I thought, that Alfie was 'emotionally disturbed' by the baby's arrival and needed attention. I remember my jaw dropping slightly as the vet imparted this diagnosis with a paternal authority that made me want to leap across the counter and do something horrible to him. I had put a lot of work into managing everyone's emotional distress at Caoimhe's arrival and subsequent diagnosis, but had still been found wanting.

We couldn't take Alfie to Ireland, so we had to find him a home. A friend and work colleague took him initially, but phoned me in tears after a few days, saying she couldn't cope. I went round and retrieved Alfie from halfway up the chimney, where he had been in hiding, keeping everyone awake with his mournful yowls. An advertisement was posted on the noticeboard at work and eventually a family came forward;

the husband was purported to be a natural with cats, a sort of feline horse-whisperer. With just a week to go, Alfie was re-housed. At that point I can honestly say I didn't care too much how he settled in. Looking back, I feel guilty about my somewhat callous attitude towards Alfie; I feel we parted with a sense of unfinished business between us which later came back to haunt me.

I went out for lots of farewell meals. I found it hard to say goodbye. I didn't know how long we'd be gone; the uncertainty left us all in a quandary. Nothing felt firm under-foot: the bedrock of friends, the garden of fruit trees, the streets I pounded with Caoimhe in her pram were disappearing like phantoms at dawn.

We held a party in the house to say goodbye and thank you. It was almost 100 years old and at one time it had been surrounded by an orchard; soon it would be tarmac and sports cars. I loved that house; its peeling white bricks had held us all together, physically and metaphorically. Over the years the breath of our laughter had grubbied the walls and here and there was a scab of Polyfilla where our anger had caused a few dents. I couldn't bear to think of a bulldozer's ball smashing into its guts.

On the last day the removalists came. The girls went to school, taking bulbs in pots as presents for their classmates. I went out for the day with Caoimhe while a team of packers in matching blue tops moved through the house like a tsunami; every crevice was filled with the rip and stick sound of their masking tape, sealing boxes. Nothing escaped their path: every sock, every pot, every painting and coat hanger was en-tombed in a cardboard cask and wheeled into oblivion. When I returned the place was a shell: no piano, no fridge or sofa or drawer filled with junk; just a dirty, dusty shell, with bright geometric shapes where the furniture had been.

I moved through the rooms feeling the coloured walls like a blind person, remembering an autumn day eight years ago, when I had come and looked around the house, calling Conor on the mobile phone to tell him delightedly, 'It's huge!' There had been a pile of leaves blown into the doorway crunchy as crisps like there was now. In the years that followed we had repainted the rooms: Wynnie and Caoimhe's blue, with big white clouds; Ellie's green, with butterflies and flowers. Outside we planted daffodils and jasmine; grew pumpkins and potatoes and a variety of herbs; made a children's garden; put up a swing and buried three rabbits and two guinea pigs near the cumquat tree. It was all soon to be gone.

That night I hit Ellie. It was the second time in her life I had struck her, and, just as the first time, I was mortified. I have no idea what she did to ignite my anger; it is only the punishment that makes a lasting imprint. 'Why did you do that?' she screeched, her voice high with shock. It wasn't the memory of leaving I intended her to have. We both cried.

I couldn't look back as we drove away the evening before our flight: out of the gateway, left into the street and past the local shop where the manager waved, as he always did, as we went by. I felt bloated with silent tears all the way to our friends' house, where we would spend the night. If this was adventure I wanted none of it.

I can barely remember much about that last night, the last supper. Looking back it seems surreal, as if I wasn't there, it was my doppelgänger that dined with gusto and raised toasts.

I remember our friends going off to work the next day and me scrawling the word 'goodbye' on their daughter's blackboard. I remember Conor raking his hair as we weighed and re-weighed the baggage which was many kilos over the limit, and muttering and shaking his head. I remember Caoimhe giggling as she ran about the room chasing the dust that danced in swathes of sunlight, oblivious to the huge upheaval that was about to veer her off course; place her on a different path that could change her nationality, her accent; strip and reassemble the mechanics of her identity.

We took a taxi to the airport with the luggage straining in the boot. I tried to remember everything on the way like some maudlin memory game: the dazzle of the bay as you round the bend on Beach Road, just before the old swimming baths; those ridiculously anorexic palm trees in St Kilda that bend alarmingly in the wind; the familiar panic driving over the too-tall Westgate Bridge—all the time wondering when I would see it again.

I cried when the plane took off, unable to contain my sadness any more. The tears fell, uncontrolled and shameful as a weak bladder. As the plane accelerated along the runway, and the dried-up paddocks of Tullamarine tilted away from me, I felt a loss I had never known before.

Caoimhe loved the plane. Her delighted smile was the antidote for my sadness; we made a harmonious pair—one tearful, one laughing, as we walked endlessly up and down the aisle, all the way to Kuala Lumpur, where we stopped overnight at a hotel with a pool. It was June 9, and Ellie's ninth birthday. I gave her an address book so she could write to her friends from whom she'd been wrenched, and a digital camera. We'd had a party before we left, one with an equine theme, in anticipation of things to come. I made her a cake in the shape of a horse's head, but rather than looking festive and fun, it sat on the plate forebodingly, an echo of *The Godfather*.

The last time we had stayed in this hotel Wynnie had been a toddler, with curly hair and ripe cheeks that were pinched and patted at every turn. My first moment of real pleasure on our journey was noticing that with Caoimhe it was no different: she, too, was fussed over by the Malaysian staff; her curly hair, her pale skin admired. It was reassuring to see that her babyhood was valued, that she was valued, away from the small safe enclave we had built in Melbourne.

A day and a half later we landed at Heathrow. I had mixed feelings coming down from the clouds and seeing the green watercolour landscape of southern England below. It didn't feel like a homecoming, more like a summoning; the holiday was over and I was being called back. And I was late.

I half expected to be greeted by my mother looking at her watch—It's been ten years! What on earth were you doing!—as we stepped into the chaotic grey world of Heathrow's arrivals hall. I was furtive as we passed quickly to the domestic terminal and boarded a plane for Dublin. I relaxed only when we were back up in the clouds, my natural home.

I have always loved Dublin airport: still small enough to retain a sense of excitement about it; no one yet seems bored by travel. I love the way Irish people clap when the plane lands, as if the pilot has accomplished some remarkable and unexpected feat. Coming through the barrier the girls saw their small cousins for the first time, waving balloons and clutching bags of sweets. Conor's brother and his wife were there; and Conor's dad, thinner than I remembered, but physically there, like he has always been.

We drove to Dundalk; my first memory is the euphoric pleasure of the countryside: hedges blotched scarlet and white with poppies and strung with lacy cow parsley; up above a powder blue sky which seemed smaller than the Australian one, and cluttered with clouds, like a room overstuffed with sofas.

We stayed with Conor's parents for two weeks while looking for a house in or around Holywood, County Down. It was not an easy time: days were spent wading through a fug of anxiety and loss as well as the pleasure of reunion; we were mourning Australia and concerned about the future. These feelings pricked away like pins and needles and formed a perpetual backdrop to the small talk and acute interest in weather patterns.

We rented the second house that we looked at. Conor found it on the Internet and it was love at first sight, mainly because it reminded us of our house in Australia—old, white and crumbling at the edges, set in a huge garden with a pond and a summerhouse and a mass of unpruned roses. It was very cheap; we soon learned why—like our house in Australia it was on death row. We took it anyway, hoping once again that plans would be delayed.

And so we began to piece our life back together, creating routines and rhythms to give back a cadence to our day. I returned to writing this book; Conor to his PhD; after the long and shapeless summer holidays where we impatiently fumbled about discovering where to buy socks, or shoes, or gluten-free bread, the girls started at the Rudolf Steiner School, half-way up the hills in Holywood, overlooking Belfast Lough.

They were very brave that first day, walking into school with a quiet dignity that masked stomachs full of jumping frogs; my eyes stung at their courage. They didn't love their new school immediately, but they tolerated it. They missed the sun and the expansive brown grass playground they were used to. They were tanned faces next to pale freckled ones, with accents straight out of *Home and Away*. They settled in and made friends, but Ellie took a while to adjust to losing her teacher in Australia, whom she had been with for three years. Conor and I loved the new school right from the start: the European flavour of its families; the rich soup of accents at drop-off time; the friendliness and the sheer bravery of the place and what it stood for—a beacon of diversity and alternative thinking in a landscape frayed by conservatism and bigotry.

———

We spent the weekends, when it wasn't raining, exploring the wild primitive beauty of North Down. We barbecued on the shores of the loughs and grappled with our flimsy fold-up stroller on wild coastal walks, trying to feel like people from a Van Morrison song.

Those were the nice bits but they were marred by the ugly stain of politics: we moved in shortly before July 12—Orange Day—when the pyres were evident and flags were flying in a loud and obnoxious proclamation of ownership and victory. I bought an old second-hand piano from a man who stored his bibles in the piano stool. One hot day Conor and his brother and brother-in-law, who was visiting from America, loaded the piano into the man's trailer and brought it to our house. Afterwards we all stood drinking beer on the patio, Catholics and Protestants engaged in cautious, polite conversation, until the man asked, innocently enough, if we were going to the local Orange Day bonfire. It was good old family fun, apparently, like communities getting together at Christmas. Except Christmas celebrates a birth, not a massacre. We floundered for an answer. No thanks.

We drove into Belfast city, down streets hung with tatty flags, past murals of young men turgid with righteousness. In the shops there were T-shirts for sale plastered with slogans like 'How to Spot a Catholic' and 'How to Spot a Protestant' side by side; history was an old married couple, alive and livid with a veneer of humour pasted over the top. It couldn't be more different from Melbourne.

I started looking up old friends, but the memories I had stored were ten years out of date; I half expected to pick up where we left off, and in some cases that was possible, but too many times I found myself mentally folded up like a foetus while my body performed obligingly like a ventriloquist's puppet—smiling, interjecting at the right places, laughing, cracking jokes. Having Caoimhe had in some way separated me; I felt marked out, different. There were times when I felt—still—a sense of inadequacy in my friends' presence; I would look at their strong healthy children, and here was my offering: my small, flawed creature. Only with my oldest friend, who also had found herself suddenly and surprisingly slapped in the face by disability, could I exhale.

I missed Melbourne like a pain which I felt somewhere behind my navel. This, I realised after six weeks, was not a bout of gastro that was going to go away; it was an ache of grief, of longing for my past to be restored. The tribal anarchy of Belfast made me yearn for the calm civility to which, on the whole, I was accustomed; the dull Irish restaurants with their uninspired dishes which always included large dollops of coleslaw made me miss the international flavours of a cosmopolitan mecca. I mourned our friends: our substitutes for family, hand-crafted over time and built to last. Most of all I missed the silver shimmer of optimism that hung over the skyline; the brightness of a city with its face towards the sun. In Belfast, things moved slowly and suspiciously under a damp grey blanket; Conor applied for job after job, but, bafflingly, nothing materialised. I was not inspired by the local press, which reminded me of my trainee reporter days. I looked back at what we had built, what we had achieved in our ten years of living on the world's bottom, and suddenly it felt like nothing, like it had been chucked into storage with our belongings. I was back where I had started, without a job, without a profile and without money.

Except it wasn't quite like that: I had to do daily mental exercises to remind myself that the past had not been snatched from me; that I carried it with me; that the experiences of the last decade plastered my heart like posters in a teenager's bedroom. I remember a few years ago an old boyfriend dying suddenly of a heart attack. I had felt so bereft, so indignant, as if something had been torn away from me forcibly, horribly. After a few days of wandering around lost and ranting, I woke up feeling good again. He hadn't gone: he was still inside me; the experience of who he was, who we were, was still alive; now I could feel sad that he was missing, but paradoxically he had come back. I welcomed his return.

It was taking longer with Melbourne. Try as I might, I could no longer feel its pulse beating, the proof of its existence inside me; I still felt deprived, as if I was not in Ireland by choice. Our belongings were still in Australia; there were few props to give me something to hang on to.

Ironically, as well as mourning Australia, I was immersed in a love affair with Northern Ireland; it was like Caoimhe's birth all over again—the sorrow and the celebration, the loss and the gain. I found myself writing whimsical e-mails about the birdlife in the garden, the wonders of hedgerows, the thrill of hearing the lark. The good bits of my childhood were being awakened; the bits where I could gallop through beech woods and countryside being a horse, being happy.

Ellie took up horse-riding at a stable on top of the hills. From the yard, where a wind always seemed to be blowing, even in summertime, you could stare out across the Lough to the faint outline of Scotland, or look the other way and see the jagged shapes of the Mourne Mountains, Lewis's Narnia. One day we went there. It was dusky and damp and we were besieged by gnats that got ensnared in our hair, crawled down our clothes. We only stayed half an hour.

The months dripped on. It rained incessantly. We played parlour games and made lots of things out of cardboard. We taught Caoimhe hide-and-seek; she learnt to count to twenty, wrap herself in curtains and jump out with a loud 'Boo!' Eventually we grew bored and bought a video recorder, only to discover that the rest of the world had moved on and no one rented videos any more. We bought a DVD player and caught up with the times. We raced raindrops down the big French windows that overlooked a garden where it was too wet to play. In September, Caoimhe's nose started to run and continued to do so for six months solid; her face was constantly rimed with treacly snot that slimed the cushions, the couches, drying and flaking, only to be replaced by a fresh trail. On the first day of spring, Wynnie came downstairs dressed in a happy smile and a T-shirt. It was less than ten degrees. We shivered into May and out of it. Conor still couldn't find a job. He changed his shirt; his hair; shaved off his stubble; tried various ties—but nothing worked. 'Perhaps you'll never get a job,' I said, ten months after he'd started trying. 'Thanks,' he said. 'I hadn't thought of that. But I will now.'

———

The reality was we were trying to do too much: finish our respective projects; raise three girls; build a life in Northern Ireland while managing the remnants of one in Melbourne. We hovered between two hemispheres, but until we let go of one, there really was no future. But how? The six-month deadline had been and gone; after the excitement of their first cold Christmas, the girls, who had obligingly thrown themselves into life in Northern Ireland, began to get tetchy—they wanted an answer as to where we would live. Ellie, at nine, had her roots firmly in Melbourne; she loved the horses but hated the weather; missed her friends; struggled more with adjusting to a new school. 'I am a polar bear in Africa,' she told me. 'I don't fit.' I tried to talk to her, to have earnest discussions about her 'feelings', but was regularly met with a blank face. One day, while I was trying yet again to create a false intimacy, in the hope that the contents of her thoughts would spill and tumble, I noticed she was wearing a different expression. I scrutinised her face expectantly: was it sadness lurking behind her eyes, or happiness? It was neither grief, nor pleasure, nor interest. It was embarrassment.

One night, Wynnie, even-tempered and sunny by nature, cracked. I have no idea what upset her but suddenly she was crying and screaming and her small body was beetroot and knotted with grief and anger. 'You took my cat off me,' she yelled. 'You took my cat. My birthday present cat. You never liked him!'

I have never loved her more than at that minute. That fucking cat—it has nine lives and Wynnie and I have only one. The next day we bought Alfie a tartan collar, a tender greeting from Belfast. We sent the cat-whisperer family an e-mail; they sent one back, with photos. It didn't sound like Alfie was enjoying himself much either, and we could have him back if we returned to Melbourne. Wynnie was immensely reassured by this; I silently pledged to try harder.

None of this helped with our quandary of where to live. Emotionally our lives were tied up in Northern Ireland; we wanted to support Conor's parents but we didn't know how; we had flown into the midst of a family in which we had only been bit-part players for ten years. There were days when the world felt very flat and I couldn't put my finger on why; then I would remember Conor's father was ill and a sadness, razor-sharp, would puncture the grey miasma and come as a relief. Cancer is a series of steps you descend slowly. There were days when Conor and I would forget about it, couldn't see it, but it was always there, a smudge on the lens. It helped to remember. I found the amnesia of grief disorientating.

Ellie and Wynnie were used to having no family in Australia, but Caoimhe was enjoying having grandparents. She loved visiting them, and knew where she was as soon as we turned into their street. At Easter, when Conor's dad had to go into hospital, Caoimhe was puzzled; she went over to the chair where he always sits: 'Where's Caoimhe's papa?' she asked, surprised.

She was delighted when he returned; the apparatus of his illness triggered her curiosity but not fear. 'Papa! Funny nose!' she exclaimed, looking at his oxygen mask. 'Papa's a pilot,' was his amused reply.

I loved the poignancy of watching their relationship develop: one at the start of life, the other at its end. It gave a reassuringly round shape to existence, it wiped out the full stops and the joins, making it seem like a never-ending circle. At almost three, Caoimhe can cling to my knee outside the safety of her home—but I loved the ease with which she'd move around Nana and Papa's house, the way she'd put her arms up for hugs and climb onto their knees. I was watching the ordinary wonder of extended family life unfold for the first time.

It was around this point that Caoimhe made her first friend, a blond-haired blue-eyed boy called Luke, who is twice her size and robust as she is fragile. Luke's mother, Cindy, offered to mind Caoimhe one morning a week and, over the months, Luke and Caoimhe's friendship has grown and changed shape, slowly, beautifully, like evening shadows. Luke is tender around Caoimhe; he covers her with kisses and tells her he loves her; they play families together and take it in turns to hold the baby. She has become more boisterous; at home she throws things around the playroom and shouts loudly 'La-la-la-la Luuuuuuuuk!' They are opposite poles, filling each other's missing bits by some magical osmosis.

Soon Caoimhe will have another cousin. Any day now, Conor's brother and his wife are expecting their third child. I no longer feel such pangs of envy as I did with the birth of their second child just over two years ago. Perhaps I have come a long way in dealing with grief; I feel as if I've had plenty of practice. I read somewhere it takes three years to get over the shock of a diagnosis of Down's. Caoimhe turned five in June.

What I have learnt since her birth is that Down syndrome is normal. Disability is normal. What is not normal is child abuse, addiction, killing, crime. That is life gone wrong. Not Caoimhe. In a relentlessly upbeat culture it takes guts to confess to personal despair. With Caoimhe's birth I have found plenty of it and I am aware there is more to come. In this book I have tried very hard not to paper over the cracks but to sing the love song as well as the lament.

Sometimes when I look back at what I've written, I'm appalled; it's as if Caoimhe exists purely to give my life purpose, but the truth is that, to some extent, she has. I am aware her viewpoint is entirely missing from these pages, but I will speak for her until she finds her own voice, perhaps to debunk all that I have said. I recognise that my words will not offer comfort to others in my shoes, for they are about my daughter, my experience of her, which is unique. Neither do I offer this book as an antidote to the views held by some of today's ethicists and medics; I wish merely to act as a reminder that everyone is unique, and that to portray Down syndrome as a collective problem is erroneous.

––––

Sometimes I think back to the night of Caoimhe's birth; when I need strength, it is a place I like to revisit. I put on the CD that Conor made for us and I am transported to a time when we both waited at the intersection between life and death, of consciousness and unconsciousness, and I will feel strong. And I will look at her and I will remember how we were; I am stripped of any pretence of cleverness and she of her label of disability. We are nameless and shapeless, raw and new.

Since that magical Tuesday evening, when, just before midnight, we split open from each other and revealed the truth of ourselves, I have undergone an internal revolution. My life has been wrung through an industrial car wash and emerged shattered, shocked and scrubbed. I can't help but wonder at how the once-comfortable landscape of my existence has been transformed into a series of complications from which I ricochet, one to another. At the interface between each one is a space—to breathe, to pause—where I can revel in the happiness of Caoimhe's being; a place where love finds a voice.

I wish I had known three years ago what I know now. How good it could be. How perfect. In those bleak, dark days in the hospital, when her diagnosis was given and received amid awkwardness and apprehension, one of my biggest fears was that I would not like her, would be ashamed of her.

Never. Caoimhe today is as beautiful, as unblemished, as she was at the hour of her birth, before she was stamped and branded. She is bigger than any label. When I look at her I am as much in love with her as always. Familiarity and routine can blunt awareness, but there are still times when I see her and catch my breath at the sight of her face; the feeling is so intense it is painful. That pain, I know now, belongs not only to love but, to grief, to loss, to the disappointment of mortality, and it will never go away. But I don't want it to. Sadness is not the worst thing I can feel.

Conor and I remain suspended in time; we do not know if we will stay here in Northern Ireland, because we do not yet know how to let go of our life in Australia. There is no Hollywood ending for us, only real ones. Caoimhe will soon have to say goodbye to the papa she has just got to know and love; and hello to her new cousin. What I do know is that life is a continuing circle of celebration and goodbyes, that we all yearn for connection and that some of us are better at it than others. It comes easily to Caoimhe, but I am clearly handicapped. As our lives go on side by side, perhaps this is something I will learn from her: her wonderful ability to connect; to bring out the best in people; to make them feel good about themselves.

There are moments in my day now so pure and powerful that mere words will not do them justice. There is no language for love this big. Life with Caoimhe is life distilled to its purest essence: to love and be loved. Isn't that everyone's *raison d'être*? You're lucky if you find it. With Caoimhe I have discovered that true love can hide in the shadows of unexpected places; that it is elusive and that sometimes you have to search hard; that you can slip into the world and slip out of it without your lips ever really tasting it.

We are blessed, Caoimhe and I. We have made it through those first few years—the all-important ones that form the blueprint for what is to come. We are a bit bruised, a bit battered, but blessed. And so I raise a toast to us; to her; to the bright, shiny, scary future. I love you, beautiful girl.

Epilogue

On a freakishly hot day in June, six days after Caoimhe's third birthday, Conor's father passed away. It was my first taste of death close at hand and the intensity of it left an indelible imprint, just as birth does. I can still see the body lying, empty as a husk, but the room overwhelmingly filled with his presence. How does a non-practising atheist explain death to a child? Caoimhe puzzled over the absence of her papa. She walked over to his chair where he had sat all the time she had known him, and put out her hands, as if to feel his absence. At the funeral, when the priest in his pulpit talked about him being gone, she asked, 'Where?'

Where indeed. When she was three I simply said, 'Papa had died,' but now she is five this explanation is too simple. Recently, at the second anniversary mass, she asked again:

'Where is papa?'

'He died,' I said.

'But where has he gone,' she persisted.

'Heaven,' I replied, for want of a better answer.

'Where is heaven?'

'Don't know. Above the sky.'

She thought for a minute and looked at the huge stained glass window in the church, where a pale summer light refracted ribbons of weak colours.

'I like that window,' she says. And then, as an afterthought. 'Papa's happy now.'

We stayed in Northern Ireland. We made the decision a few months after the funeral. Fate played a part, I feel. Driving along one summer's evening over the bumpy Holywood hills, I stumbled across a farmhouse to rent. It was a plain white house on the crest of a bald hill, set in a whitewashed square farmyard from which the views were spectacular. The north stretched out across Belfast Lough to the faint outline of Scotland; the south was bordered by the jagged eruptions of the Mournes. On a hot stuffy afternoon in Melbourne I had somehow painted this view on an old piece of wood, born out of longing; there was even a bank of foxgloves and poppies bordering the farmyard. It was meant to be.

The girls loved the house, too, not least because we shared it with seven horses and ponies, ranging from a Shetland to a thoroughbred. The property had been a pig farm in its previous incarnation and the barns were now rented out as stables. Still, an overwhelming odour of pig lingered every time you opened a barn door; as a person who has never been able to joyfully embrace a plate of ham, it felt rather strange to share my home with the ghosts of several hundred porkers. We called our new home 'Piggery Heights' in their honour.

I loved being surrounded by fields. That autumn we collected bulging buckets of blackberries from the hedgerows which bubbled into jam on the stove top in the farmhouse kitchen. We watched thousands of starlings gather in the tree by the barn and take off into the purple dusk and morph into noisy viscous shapes. Winter brought rain and mud and an endless pile up of sodden garments and glistening boots left by the back door. And the wind, when it came, stayed for months; a squatter, a poltergeist that screamed around the doors and windows and was tolerated under sufferance, as one puts up with an aged relative, or paying guest, who simply cannot be shifted.

Winter also bought unexpected blankets of snow, sudden as mirage and prone to disappear as quick. The girls went sledging, but Caoimhe, bundled up like a bag of Oxfam clothing, hated it. She couldn't stand the cold; her stiff fingers couldn't be prised into gloves that stayed put and her nose ran more than ever. In winter she sort of hibernated; her movements became slower and the endless respiratory infections caused her to regress back to babyhood. We spent too many hours together in front of *The Tweenies*. To brighten the gloom of winter we bought two Cavalier King Charles puppies, rather impetuously, from a woman from Enniskillen who met us in a car park at some faceless trading estate outside Belfast, where she produced them from the boot of her car. It was love at first sight for Ellie and Wynnie and Lily and Lucy when we came home to Piggery Heights.

Love grew slowly for Caoimhe. At first she was terrified of the puppies' exuberance; their endless licking and bounding, the fury of their brown and white tails banging her unstable legs. But over time they became her best friends and today they are inseparable; every morning she sits in their pen and converses and they listen patiently and adoringly, licking her cheek lovingly at all the right intervals. They are customers in her shop; the pupils in her school; the comforters for her tears; they are always on her side. They have become indispensable.

Spring took a long time to emerge from the winter onslaught. Slowly patches of yellow shone out of the endless grey and green as the gorse bust into colour; celandines and primroses appeared by the roadside and the wind hushed its noise. Winter wheat began shooting up in the field behind the house and the dogs enjoyed a daily gallop through the damp brown furrows. As the weeks progressed, swallows arrived; raining down like black bullets; in the evening dusk they swooped low in and out of the barns feasting on the clouds of midges that hung around the horse dung. Pale sun bleached the yellow to white, as buckthorn, then hawthorn and cow parsley filled the hedgerows, heralding the promise of summer.

Except it never really arrived. There were days when you'd think it was just about to happen; when the sun would have some fire in it, and the world was washed in weak shadows; but the next day it would peter out like a damp squib. Every day we'd hold our breath thinking could this be the start of a warm dry spell, but it was only ever teasing. The heat was like medicine that we just couldn't obtain; without it, Caoimhe seemed to be in a state of chronic respiratory discomfort.

We headed for France, starved so we were, of the blast of hot dry heat we'd gotten so used to in Australia. Caoimhe struggled with the change to her routine; my greatest memory is of driving to the beach in Biarritz, or the towns of Bayonne and Pau, accompanied by the Tweenies. It was the thing that reminded her of home; and she was happiest in the car listening to the familiar songs. The rest of us would groan as the ignition started, the CD slid in and the whine of Jake, or the shrill bossiness of Bella, blasted through the speakers, but the sound of her homesickness was worse. And at least her nose stopped running.

That autumn, as the swallows gathered on the wire, Caoimhe started pre-school. This was an ordeal; the Steiner school she was attending was concerned they would not be able to meet her needs. 'Is she continent?,' I was asked by the pre-school teacher—a question which I found mortifying, as it was delivered in front of a group of other mothers. There were delays whilst the school decided whether or not they were able to accept her during which we looked at state schools. But the site of small children in grey uniforms gathered around tables laden with maths books made me shudder; Caoimhe would surely be lost in such a sea of grey. I hoped that at least at the Steiner school she would be more visible.

Her year there was not an easy one. She never willingly embraced school for many reasons, the main one being that she simply wasn't ready. She was the youngest in her class but the education laws insisted that children her age had to be in school; there were no exceptions. The class was very small— only eight children including two other girls who lived next door to each other and were like sisters. Caoimhe stood no chance of breaking into their fantasy world and as a child hampered by social anxiety anyway, it dented her confidence more. Luke, her first friend, remained loyal and kind to her but naturally gravitated towards the other boys, whose robustness and energy terrified Caoimhe. She spent too much time on her own. Because the school was not state funded she didn't receive classroom help and her assessment scores were high enough not to warrant it anyway. But although her vocabulary matched an average four-year-old, emotionally she needed a lot of help.

What saved her that year was her close attachment to a new carer; a mother at the school who had a child one year younger than Caoimhe. Erin became her second true friend. Caoimhe loved going to Erin's house; dressing up and playing pirates, princesses, doctors, shops. On dry days they would go to the park and the ice-cream bar and eat cones smothered in multi-coloured hundreds and thousands which got everywhere and glued her curls together. She always came home smiling. In this small world, this microcosm, she flourished. She was loved and she knew it.

She continued to surprise me, to toss out my lingering out-dated preconceptions, like mouldy old bread. On the door of her bedroom is her name in colourful wooden letters. Occasionally, I would spell them out for her. One day, shortly before her fifth birthday, she said to me, 'Mummy, I can spell my name . . . C.A.O.I.M.H.E.' and then she threw herself open with laughter at the pleasure of seeing my gob-smacked face. Conor was right to stick with her name. Of course she can spell it. I am ashamed to think I thought she never would.

On another occasion, when she was watching one of her beloved Barney videos, she saw one of his plastic child followers hopping. Caoimhe was intrigued. She watched it again and again. Then she had a go herself. She fell over. She got up and tried again. She fell over. 'Mummy I can't do it,' she yelled, puffed up with fury before crumpling like a blown crisp bag. I held her limp body until the sobs subsided and she was ready to try again. And again. By the end of the week she could hop and she hopped everywhere. In shops, in the street, to school and back. This is the secret of Caoimhe's success; her burning ambition, the rage that spurs her to keep on going. I hope it never leaves.

And so for a while our lives began to fall into place. Conor finished his PhD and got a job with a biomedical firm. I devoted myself to housewifery for the first time in my life and I was crap at it. I remember going to the local delicatessen and buying butter called Housewife's Choice and my insides lurched because this, I knew, was my future, at least, until Caoimhe was settled at school. Because of her delicate health and also because she couldn't cope with a full morning of pre-school, I would pick her up at 11 o' clock most days, so there wasn't much time to indulge in a career. Every morning I would watch Conor go off to work with a mix of relief (that he had got a job!) and envy; I missed having an office to bolt to; a paper to read in peace and the ability to purchase a meal I hadn't had to cook. I felt the absence of a career like a physical pain and threw myself into home renovations, except they didn't really help. I have never been much of a shopper; I can't stand supermarkets or shopping malls and develop a sort of amnesia as soon as I enter through the sliding glass doors. It is as if I lose track not only of time and purpose, but of who I am. I have been known to abandon my shopping trolley in the middle of an aisle and flee. At school I learnt Latin instead of Domestic Science and with hindsight, perhaps this was unwise.

I think my children missed their father's daytime presence, or at least his cooking. I buried myself in recipe books but somehow rarely managed to produce anything that all five of us would eat. I made endless lists of favourite foods only to find that the second production of a successful meal was never greeted with the same enthusiasm. Occasionally I just bought 35 ready meals for the week, as a sort of adolescent rebelliousness against my enforced kitchen enslavement. Caoimhe's diet was easy enough; it consisted of soup and oat biscuits and homemade juice, yoghurt, chocolate and the occasional sausage. Nothing else. We considered it ground-breaking when she started to eat pasta but that was short-lived.

Despite my maladjustment to domestic slavery, there was much about life in Northern Ireland that I began to cherish. In some ways I felt a sort of affinity to Belfast, bruised and battered but mercifully still standing. What I noticed, coming from Australia, is how accepted Caoimhe was. Nobody stared at her; in the dreaded shopping centres she blended into the landscape of pale faces and animated children with ease. I see many more wheelchairs here than I ever did in Melbourne, where perfection is prized and lifestyle all-consuming. I ponder over the paradox of a country torn apart by its inability to accept religious difference that can display such a tolerance towards human difference. Conversely, religion which has caused such bloodshed and polarity may unify a belief that all children have a right to life. Abortion, I discover, is a grey area here; the North never embraced the 1967 Abortion Act, but women have more rights than they do in the South where it is illegal full stop. It seems to be the one area on which all major political parties share agreement; that abortion should be kept at bay.

I have softened my attitudes, I think. Somehow in my journey towards total acceptance of Caoimhe I have learned tolerance. One day I am walking with Caoimhe and the two dogs, Lily and Lucy, around a duck pond. We get talking to a woman who admired firstly the dogs, then my child, as the Irish tend to do. Lily starts to cough and the woman stares down at her, as she stands spluttering away, next to Caoimhe in her stroller.

'What's wrong with her,' she asks abruptly.

'Kennel Cough,' I reply. 'Really nasty dose. Tried everything, but she's on the mend, thank God. You should see the vet bills.'

She stares at me. 'I meant your little girl.'

'Oh!' I was caught off guard. And for the first time since being here I am transported in an instant back to the doctor's surgery in Melbourne and the GP's sympathetic comment on seeing Caoimhe: 'Bad luck.' But this time the words don't hurt nearly as much.

I see tolerance in my other daughters and their friends too. Occasionally we would join our friends at their cottage on Inis Meáin, and it is here some of my best memories regarding Caoimhe have been cultivated; pearls that hold the threads together. Rewind the tape and I see her with her sisters, Ellie and Wynnie, Luke, and his brother Oscar, in the kitchen during a rain shower. Outside, while the great grey clouds bear down on the sea, a play is being enacted, a game conjured up. The patience that is bestowed on Caoimhe as the rules are ex-plained, the parts given out, catch me in the throat. Here in this kitchen there is safety and freedom in acceptance; she is welcomed into their games out of love and not pity, which I have always dreaded. Her heightened sense of humour, her ability to mimic, gives her direct access into the mystical world of childhood if people would only take the time to understand her. Back on Inis Meáin, she will catch Luke's eye and tell him: 'Your hair looks like a turkey,' and they will both collapse in giggles.

Occasionally Wynnie asks questions about her sister's con-dition and I answer as truthfully as I dare. Wynnie is the one who is closer in age to Caoimhe and who often bears the brunt of her sister's fury and frustration. There are times when I feel very sorry for her. When she recently asked me if she would have a child with Down syndrome, I thought I was being reassuring when I replied: 'It's very unlikely.'

'That's a pity,' she replied. 'I guess you've got to be lucky.'

I was taken aback. All I could offer was a weak smile. 'Guess you do.'

For three years we tried very hard to make life in the North work. We dug a vegetable plot and planted potatoes, broccoli, peas, beans and strawberries. I daubed the yard with hanging baskets stuffed with trailing geraniums and nasturtium and cultivated a wild flower garden of sorts. Caoimhe learned to feed the ponies, shrieking with delight when their hairy lips brushed against her flat hand. We visited Conor's family in the South and wondered at the difference in lifestyle crossing an invisible border. After his father died we planted a row of tiny saplings in his memory. These are the roots we have put down but somehow we still feel rootless. Here in Northern Ireland, we only have the present; there is no sense of past. I cannot show the girls where they took their first steps, had their first haircut; we are linked to this place by the single thread of Steiner education.

Inevitably when cracks began to appear at the school, it felt like a mini-earthquake beneath our feet. Caoimhe wasn't really thriving, and neither were her sisters. The school was undergoing major changes which were unsettling and created animosity between various parents that bled into the classroom and upset the children. It got to the stage where we had to remove them for their own safety. By some miracle of timing, a job opportunity arose in Australia for Conor and the pieces began to fall into place.

And so the circle is complete. We will return to Melbourne when autumn begins its decay, which seems apt. September is spring time in Melbourne, when the jasmine hedges burst into flower and the pungent scent spills into the streets.

I hope that Caoimhe's health will be better; that she will uncurl her body, bent in defence against the climate; that once the polyester layers are peeled off she will stretch and grow and revel in the warmth that will put pay to any lingering viruses that thrive in this continual damp. I hope this, in some way, will buffer her against the pain she will feel at leaving her Nana, her uncles who have bestowed on her the best sort of love, her friends and mine, who have suffused her in different warmth. The wrench will be huge. I worry about returning to a country where people with disability are pretty much in-visible; where Caoimhe's appearance once attracted so many comments, well-meaning or otherwise.

I know that I will miss the rawness of the countryside, the daily battle with the elements which brings its own sense of satisfaction. I will long for the wind on the wheat field, the way the stems bend like Muslims in prayer, towards a faceless god that exists beyond the break in the clouds. I will miss the mewing buzzards that surf the air currents, the larks that startle and rise from the jungle of wheat as you pass through; the white horse, pale as a ghost, cropping a moonlit field. There will be times on a baking hot day in the middle of cramped, congested Melbourne when I will close my eyes against the burn of tears and longing for a life that is over in the real sense, but one that I carry with me and will revisit, time and time again.

I remember when we first moved to Belfast from Australia, people used to eye us suspiciously. 'Why on earth did you come here?' they would ask. 'You must be mad.'

Perhaps we are.

References

CHAPTER 3

Bondo, U, Ida, *Life with My Handicapped Child*, Faber and Faber, UK, 1980.

Kanat, J, *Bittersweet Baby*, Compcare, USA, 1987.

Newton, Dr R, *The Down's Syndrome Handbook*, Vermilion, UK, 2004.

Selikowitz, M, *Down Syndrome: the Facts*, Oxford University Press, USA, 1997.

Stray-Gundersen, K, *Babies with Down Syndrome*, Woodbine House, USA, 1986.

Ward, O Conor, 'John Langdon Down: the man and the message', *Down Syndrome Research and Practice*, Vol 6, Issue 1, UK, 1999.

Wright, D, *Mental Disability in Victorian England: the Earlswood Asylum 1847-1901*, Oxford University Press, UK, 2001.

CHAPTER 4

Cocchi, R, 'Is there any seasonal influence in the conceptions of Down's syndrome subjects?', *Italian Journal of Intellective Impairment*, Vol 2, Issue 1, Italy, 1989.

CHAPTER 6

Burkeman, O, 'Baby-learning videos lack educational value, say American psychologists', *The Guardian*, UK, May 2006.

Costa, Dr A, 'Why Do We Need More Support for Research in Down Syndrome?', Mile High Down Syndrome Association, USA: www.mhdsa.org

Down's Syndrome Association, *Access to Education*, Down's Syndrome Association Publication, UK, 2004.

Gottlieb, L, 'I bought my baby at the sperm bank', *Sunday Times*, UK, August 2005.

Hill, A, 'Educational toys? An old box teaches just as much', *The Observer*, UK, September 2005.

Pennisi, E, 'Cell Biology: Gene Linked to Down Syndrome Retardation', *Science*, USA, December, 1996.

CHAPTER 7

Cunningham, C, 'Families of Children with Down Syndrome', *Down Syndrome Research and Practice*, Vol 4, Issue 3, 1996.

Van Riper, M, 'Living with Down Syndrome: the Family Experience', *Down Syndrome Quarterly*, USA, Vol 4, Num 1, March 1999.

CHAPTER 8

'A Heartbreaking Choice', www.aheartbreakingchoice.com

'Baby Dies; Physician Upheld', *Chicago Tribune*, USA, November 1915.

Black, E, 'Hitler's Debt to America', *The Guardian*, UK, February 2004.

Buckley, S, 'Prenatal Testing—Technological Triumph', *Byronchild*, Australia, September 2004.

De Crespigny, L and Chervenak, F, *Prenatal Tests: the Facts*, Oxford University Press, UK, 2006.

De Crespigny, L, Espie, M, and Holmes, S, *Prenatal Testing*,

Making Choices in Pregnancy, Penguin Books, Australia, 1998.

Deane, K, 'The Choice: Sophie is Our Gift', *Sunday Magazine*, Australia 2003.

Down's Syndrome Association, *He'll Never Join the Army*, Down's Syndrome Association Publication, UK, 1999.

Five Live Report, 'The Terminators?', BBC Radio, UK, September 2003.

Irwin, D and Findlay, I, 'Using Single Cell DNA Fingerprinting to Identify Fetal Cells Serially Enriched from Pap Smears', XIX International Congress of Genetics, Australia, 2003.

Kmietowicz, Z, 'Down's Children Received "Less Favourable" Hospital Treatment', *British Medical Journal*, UK, April 2001.

Marsh, B and Day, E, News Review, *The Sunday Telegraph*, UK, May 2006.

Mealey, R, 'Down's Syndrome and Genetic Cleansing', PM Archive, ABC, Australia, March 2000.

Ney, P and Peters, M, 'Eugenics and Down's Syndrome', www.messengers2.com, USA, May 2000.

Rapp, R, *Testing Women, Testing the Fetus*, Routledge, USA, 1999.

Savulescu, J, 'New science, enhancement of human beings and the future of medicine', National Press Club National Australia Bank Address, Australia, June 2005.

Savulescu, J, 'Resources, Down's syndrome and cardiac surgery', *British Medical Journal*, UK, April 2001.

Scott, C, 'Relative Values', *The Sunday Times* Magazine, UK, October 2006.

Singer, P, *Rethinking Life and Death*, Oxford University Press, UK, 1994.

'Will £1000 get you an Alpha Baby?', *Grazia*, UK, April 2006.